BOWIE
CHANGES

THE ILLUSTRATED DAVID BOWIE STORY

Omnibus Press
London/New York/Sydney/Cologne

Exclusive distributors:

Book Sales Limited
78 Newman Street, London W1P 3LA, UK

The Putnam Publishing Group
200 Madison Avenue, NY, NY10016, USA

Omnibus Press
139 King Street, Sydney, NSW 2000, Australia

To the Music Trade Only:
Music Sales Limited
78 Newman Street, London W1P 3LA, UK

Music Sales Corporation
799 Broadway, NY, NY10003, USA

Book designed by Mike Bell
Picture research by Valerie Boyd
Typeset by Capital Letters

First published 1980 Omnibus Press.
Second edition published 1982.
Third edition, revised and updated by Chris Charlesworth, published 1983.

Omnibus Press
(A division of Book Sales Limited)

ISBN 0.86001.772.9
UK Order No. OP 40880

Printed in England by JB Offset Printers (Marks Tey) Limited, Marks Tey, Essex

CONTENTS

WE PASSED UPON THE STAIR AN INTRODUCTION

To say that David Bowie is a man of ch-ch-changes, would be a cliché, and I won't miss the opportunity. From his early days at Bromley Tech, in South London, learning the saxophone and wanting to be a star, through the swinging sixties in swingin' London, dragging himself through the many faces of the music industry; playing at being Tony Newley, or Bob Dylan or Marc Bolan, David Bowie's record of failure was almost unsurpassed: eleven flop singles and two flop albums with no less than seven record companies!

One of David Bowie's problems during the early phase of his career, those six years running about being three different types of artist at the same time, was that the years between 1963 and 1969 saw such a dramatic change in the business that it was all a poor boy could do to keep up with it and keep taking the pills; if Bowie's changes can have been said to have come from anywhere they must have come from looking around him and watching the development of the music scene.

When David left school, the heroes of the time were the rebels of rock and roll but by the beginning of the sixties many of the classic American rock and rollers had become sanitised to appeal to a mature audience. The army had processed Elvis Presley, Buddy Holly was dead and, in England, Cliff Richard had turned into an MOR singer via Christianity. Artists like Tony Newley, Max Bygraves and Frank Ifield wore suits and attracted the parents of the kids who yearned for more aggressive music.

But on the fringes of these two musical styles were vast numbers of 'minority' styles which were gathering popularity and it was within these styles that the kids of David's age were seeking their expression.

Jazz had always been popular, and David had flirted with it while at school, but jazz was being pushed sideways by a new wave of several little movements which were regarded in those days as mere flashes in the pan, and the groups as "eight-day-wonders" (as many of them were). Folk was enjoying a revival in the US and was filtering over to the UK with the records of Bob Dylan and Joan Baez as the intellectuals and students left the jazz cellars for the road to Aldermaston and anti-nuclear protest marches organised by the CND, and Britain spawned its own folk heroes in the form of Donovan, but while David Jones flirted with Folk he was aware that it wouldn't be enough to make him a star; and anyway Folk was a participatory thing where the audience expect to get involved . . . Dylan realised this himself in 1965 and picked up an electric guitar.

Rhythm 'n' Blues (r 'n' b) was also coming up as were other electrified styles. Groups like The Rolling Stones were bursting upon the scene and making their fortunes almost overnight, and then there were The Beatles with their own rock 'n' roll-r 'n' b based Anglified string of hits in the charts. It was to these groups that the young David Jones was drawn. However, the record companies were treating them very much as eight-day-wonders, in the same way as they regarded skiffle (which was an eight day fad).

And then there were the other minor

styles which sprung up and were rapidly absorbed into the mainstream as it became clear that rock music was not going to be just-a-here-today affair but that a revolution had taken place, and that these kids were the future of the record industry. Mod, Heavy Metal, Acid Rock, etc were all to be accepted and become part of a diverse range of styles the public could choose from.

There lay the main problem; which style to follow? David seemed to be running to keep in step. By necessity anyone who is following cannot be a field leader, and Bowie just kept following along, changing styles as anyone would change clothes, each record showed him trying to jump on the prevailing bandwagon and slipping off.

During this confusing time for the young Bowie, there was always his manager, Ken Pitt, standing in the background, helping try to keep the road open in front of David. Sometimes this help was a hindrance; David's Tony Newley phases for instance, Pitt was convinced that the way to make out in the record industry was to be a 'trouper', an all round artist who could turn to the stage or pantomime in lean times. To do this the artist had to have a following among the older mums and dads, and to have this following he had to be clean cut and demonstrate the breadth of his talent, and artists like Tony Newley and Tommy Steele had the respect of the industry and the older age bracket following. So it was into the studio to record à la Newley on a series of mindless and sometimes quirky little numbers (which of course got nowhere!). It is to Pitt's credit that he managed Bowie totally, when the going got rough he was still able to convince people in the business that his artist would make it one day, he didn't walk out on his kid, but hung on in there, pulling record contracts out of the hat like rabbits.

Pitt was not dealing with a machine; it is too easy to forget that Bowie was a teenager and had to 'find out about life' and himself. Pitt also had to cope with David growing up, and this was not a smooth transition.

London was swinging, and David, on the fringe of the music industry which was the centre of the 'swinging scene', was supposed to be a part of this groovey new movement (and you can't be that if you are a Tony Newley clone). David played the young mod about town finding converts, opening the bill for The Who in the heartland of Swinging London: Soho.

As the smartness of mod gave way to the stoned hippy days, David also rolled up his shirt sleeves and waded into it emerging with long hair and tie-dye T-shirt. But Bowie wasn't alone in this; it was another fashion (or movement) and The Beatles and Rolling Stones did their bit too, but did it better than Bowie – both artistically and financially.

These days of hash and music grew directly out of the economic boom of the mid sixties which gave the kids their first taste of freedom from their parents' pocket money . . . their money was their own and they would spend it whichever way they wanted in order to make their lives their own, and perhaps they would find the meaning of life . . . trips to India and Buddhism were in vogue at the time as the youth of Britain (and the Western world for that matter) got out of their heads and saw that the old values of working hard to be a statistic with the required semi, wife and 2.5 children, was not quite such a good goal as it had always been made out to be . . . individuality was the key. Hash was our drug, we – the youth – had discovered it (it had been around for about 5,000 years but what the hell . . .) and we were going to change our minds and set the world free. It was an age of slogans about freedom and other such abstract concepts for the Western children of this revolution.

It was something Bowie couldn't ignore. Much to Pitt's chagrin, he couldn't fit into the Newley all-round-entertainer straitjacket which his manager was always trying to push him into. The music industry was changing and the old values no longer held the respect which they once had. The business-suited company business men were now passing their jobs over to younger long haired turned-on and tuned-in (if not dropped out) smart-asses who were close to the public in age and attitudes and could detect minor shifts in public taste. This new breed of record executive was not impressed by someone who could sound like Tony Newley (who by this time wasn't selling records anyway). They wanted someone who could express the meaning of life (or sound like it) who was in touch with the public. While Bowie was in touch, Pitt wasn't.

The late sixties' hippy movement placed Art highly in their priorities, but like the movement itself, the appreciation was not in a rigid frame, but in free expression. Bowie reverted to the hinterland to indulge in a little free expression. Back in Bromley he started something for himself; an arts-lab. Something he could be responsible for, something he could do for himself without the guiding hand of his manager, Ken Pitt. The Arts Lab at the Three Tuns in Beckenham wasn't much but it was probably the first thing which Bowie had done for himself . . . and although he didn't earn any money that wasn't the object, it was a self discovery voyage. He got involved in mime and dance, played life like he was a small town Dylan and came out to fill the contracts which Pitt had magicked up for him back in the centre of London.

These contracts were acquired on the basis of Bowie's songwriting ability and not on his ability to mimic Newley. He still didn't get the real breaks, but he was happy with his Arts Lab and his small circle of friends like Marc Bolan and Rick Wakeman, who were also struggling on the fringe of the music scene.

Even when he had his 'big' hit *Space Oddity*, he blew it; he couldn't cope with the stardom which he was shot into . . . whether it was because of the drugs he was taking (eleven years after the hit another song took him into the charts which had the line 'we know Major Tom's a junkie') or whether it was that he had been smashing his head against the charts for six years and when success came it frightened him, doesn't matter.

The biggest change Bowie ever made was in getting rid of Ken Pitt as a manager. Good and faithful as Pitt was, he wasn't the manager to make David Bowie a star. What was needed was a sharp young go-ahead manager of the new breed . . . this he found in the man who took him out of the Ken Pitt management contract; Tony DeFries.

DeFries pushed Bowie into a confident artist's frame of mind, which gave rise to Ziggy Stardust . . . the Man . . . and the STAR. It is this point where most people came into Bowie's career.

The concept of singing about the rise to stardom of a fictional character must have been drawn from Bowie's observations around the scene; but it was the perfect vehicle for Bowie to play the star (without being presumptuous: he wasn't presuming to be a star, he was acting out the part of Ziggy Stardust and making him credible).

But Bowie *became* a star through Ziggy Stardust, he carried him around with him to interviews, and he was interviewed as Ziggy, the Star!

There is no denying that Bowie's music had by this time found a direction, a style in which he felt comfortable, there were the various little media hypes to help him along the way, the limos, the fancy hotels, the big promotional budgets etc. But what had happened was that in the mist surrounding his soul-seeking he had developed a style which was his own. He was creating one of the fads which he used to follow hoping to jump onto the stage and copy, he was now being copied, not only by other artists but by the kids in the street who latched onto him as the new leader, in music and in fashion . . . and if anything can be thought of as being the secret of his success at this time it was this reversal of the role.

But he had only started, he was caught out as Ziggy, and nobody knew better than he did that the music scene changes almost every year, new groups come up and others are forgotten, the eight-day-wonders. In order to survive he had to change; not following the pack, but he had to lead it; come up with something new every time, every album, in order to stay at the top.

So we saw the emergence of the Bowie style of changing image with every album, constantly veering off into new music styles, each change was total, he looked different, sounded different as he stormed his way through the album charts (which by this time had become as important as the single charts).

Eventually all of this constant pressure to stay on top must get dull, as it becomes the very rat-race which was despised in the late sixties. Is it any wonder that Bowie should start pleasing himself; he wasn't trying to be an artist, now he was one, and wanted his artistic freedom which he was overlooking in order to run in the race . . . it was time to slow down.

The changes came slower now, they weren't so dramatic as he eased himself into electronic music with Brian Eno, and has been in to ever since . . . not the most popular of musical styles in which to find himself again . . . but what he wanted to do, where he saw himself being creative and not just a star hit-machine. The signs are now that he's moving out of the more abstract musical end of electronic music and returning to a lyrical vocal form of expression.

Having made the grade he didn't need the prying eyes of the world looking into his living room anymore, and withdrew into himself, and his small clique of friends, cutting himself off from the media. He has a right to that and apart from the skimpiest facts gleaned from interviews the latter part of his career is just a series of album listings with the occasional single or public appearance, while the earlier part is more accessible. It has been treated that way in this discography. Bowie wanted to be in the public eye and his life therefore was in the public domain, it's the price he had to pay, later he wanted his privacy and he had earned it.

This book contains many references to bootleg records and tapes. All of which are illegal. They may be valid insights into an artist's style or direction, or give the hungry public more than the artist wants them to have – without giving the artist the financial credit for selling the product. There is no place in a discography such as this for a moral stance about these bootlegs, they do draw conflicting emotions from the author; they are a rip off, *and* they are the source of some insight into the artist . . . they do exist and as such cannot and must not be ignored. They are therefore treated as 'historical recordings'.

Be Warned: Bootlegs are illegal and bootleggers operate underground. There are just as many sharks underground as there are anywhere else, and there are no consumer protection laws underground, so if you, the reader, must buy bootlegs prepare to be ripped off and do not re-record them to sell or trade (other than to very close friends) because you will get busted.

I'd like to thank vast numbers of people who helped me in one way or another to put this discography together. Some of them are: Trevor Byfield for the albums and drink, Ken Denham for his direction finding advice, Barb & Jayne at M.S. for being there, Bob Wise for his strange ashtray and M.S., Musique Boutique for being a great little shop, Gordon Swanson for his cynicism 'you've been here before', DoDo and Blue for being so fast. Also to The Man who sold the world . . . dum dum de dum . . .

Stuart Hoggard, London 1980

SOMEBODY UP THERE LIKES ME

Bromley Tech has one real claim to fame; it had a teacher back in the early sixties by the name of Frampton who was organising the 1962 Christmas pageant; his son played in a pop group who called themselves The Little Ravens; they knew another group at college and shared the bill that Christmas with George and the Dragons. George and the Dragons had a cool saxophonist, fifteen year-old David Jones – the very one who went on to fame and fortune as David Bowie!

Such are the stories of the pop industry of the time, a regular teenager's dream! The other kid, Peter Frampton, went on to become Pete Frampton 'The Face' of 1967, as guitarist with Humble Pie, and later made it on his own . . . but that's another story, file it under Peter & The Wolf and forget it – this story is about little David Jones and how he took the music business by storm eight years after his college bop and became an idol for millions of fans world-wide.

David Jones was born the son of Haywood Stenton Jones and Margaret Mary Burns at 40, Stansfield Rd, Brixton on January 8, 1947 (not 1946 as has often been quoted – David would often claim to be a year older than he really was, as much for vanity as for contractual reasons). His parents were living together without benefit of clergy because Haywood was waiting for a divorce from his first wife, Hilda Louise. Margaret already had a seven year old son by a previous marriage, Terry, by the time young David was born. The family lived in Brixton for the next eight years while Haywood worked for Dr. Barnardo's Homes.

Brixton is now one of the arse ends of London, a decaying sprawl of middle-class Victorian three storey houses split up into flats when the Victorian middle-classes moved out. The early fifties saw the first groups of West Indians moving into the area right off the boat from Jamaica looking for the land of plenty they had all been told of . . . what they found was Brixton, the only place they could afford to colonise, it is now one of the many black ghettoes of London. David Bowie remembers it much the way it was and is, deprived, with some kids going to school in the shadow of Brixton prison with the clothes hanging off their backs, although he is quick to point out that he was one of the lucky ones who always left home after a hearty breakfast.

At the age of eight, David and his fifteen-year-old brother, Terry, were sent out of London to an uncle's farm in Yorkshire where they spent two years in the country before returning to their parents who by now had moved to a suburb eight miles out of the city, Bromley.

David was always being influenced by his elder brother in the way young brothers tend to be; Terry's main interest was music and in particular jazz. It was the time of the 'beat generation' and Terry gave his kid brother Kerouac's *On The Road* and Ginsberg's *How!* to read while still at school and it was through Terry that he chose to learn sax. Terry got the wanderlust before David was out of school and like a British Kerouac signed on as a merchant seaman and took off.

Beyond Terry, David had his own group of friends at school, all of whom had similar musical leanings, his best mate was George Underwood, but this friendship didn't stop them fighting over a girl David fancied but who was going out with George. During the fight Underwood landed a punch on Jones' eye . . . suddenly blood started gushing out of it and David was rushed off to hospital, his pupil had been paralysed and he almost lost his sight. This old playground war wound never really cleared up and the left eye is still paralysed.

Out of hospital a couple of months

later, still the best of friends despite it all, David and George put a 'beat' group together called George and The Dragons.

'David had already become quite a hero at school,' said Frampton later about the Christmas gig. 'He used to bring his sax to school and it was generally known that he had spent three years learning to play it.' The school choir sang from 'Oklahoma!' the lost property lady sang *There's A Hole in My Bucket* before the Little Ravens came on followed by George and The Dragons. Frampton recalls that the audience were clapping and cheering the kid with the sax as he smoothed about the stage.

He may have been a hero with the kids at school but on an academic level he was almost a bust, he left in 1963 with only two O-levels in Art and Woodwork.

He got a job on leaving school in an advertising agency as a commercial artist (this part of the story seems a little vague, since David jokes and dodges the question when asked about this particular bit of his life . . . but normally Ad. agencies only take on Art College graduates as commercial artists and an O-level in art is not an A-level and a college diploma short of that . . . whatever the story he had 'tripped on with capitalism' and left after six months), working during the day got in the way of his late night jazz sessions anyway.

In the middle of 1963 all hell broke loose on the music scene and we are still feeling the repercussions today; The Beatles. Apart from introducing a new sound into the British pop charts, The Beatles made jazz obsolete among kids David Jones' age. David promptly dropped his jazz and took up the next step towards pop, R 'n' B, with a group of four other Bromley kids he had met 'in a barber shop'. They formed a group called The King Bees and played around the clubs in ever increasing circles from Bromley without much success, since, although the record companies were running around signing up groups who might rival the ten day wonders EMI had picked up in The Beatles, they were looking North to Liverpool, and Bromley is South of London.

A big name in the papers around that time was John Bloom, a self-made flamboyant tycoon who made the papers gloriously when his multi-million-pound empire based around Rolls Razors (no relation to Rolls Royce), crashed sometime later. Bloom was young, go-ahead and on the fringe of the music scene, holding parties attended by various Beatles and other sixties stars such as Alma Cogan and The Beverley Sisters. The press said that he was splashing his money around, and David Jones thought that it would be a good idea if he splashed a little in the direction of The King Bees and wrote telling him this. Bloom must have been amused because he replied by telegram pointing out that *actual* involvement in the music business was not his business but that Jones should contact Les Conn.

David did and was asked to play at Bloom's wedding anniversary party; as a party band they were a flop; turning up at Bloom's ever-so-smart party in jeans and sweat-shirts to play r 'n' b (which hadn't quite taken off yet); 'Most of the guests just ignored us and carried on talking as though we weren't there,' David later recalled. Dejected, they legged it back to Bromley.

The next day the news wasn't all bad, on the contrary Conn had big news. There was a feeling in the music scene that The Beatles and groups like them were on their way out, the public seemed to have had their fill of them and of all the soundalikes over the eighteen months they had been saturating the charts. The public were looking for something new . . . and the something they were going to get (for the next eighteen months at least) was r 'n' b . . . Decca already had The Rolling Stones and Conn had managed to persuade them that The King Bees could give them the monopoly on the 'new wave' . . . particularly as they were looking stupid having turned The Beatles down when they were offered to them.

It was a result of this feeling that Conn soon had The King Bees along at Decca with contracts signed ready to whisk them off on the road to stardom in 1964.

June 1964
LIZA JANE/LOUIE LOUIE GO HOME
Vocalion-Pop V9221 (re-released September 1978, Decca F13807).
The King Bees: David Jones, Bob Allen, Dick Underwood, Frank Howard, Roger Bluck.
Producer: Les Conn.

The A side was written and produced by Les Conn, while the B side was a re-hash of a minor 'hit' by Paul Revere & The Raiders earlier that year.

The single went nowhere and David resorted to playing in two groups at the same time in order to cover the nights when one of the bands couldn't get a booking, the alternative to The King Bees was The Manish Boys.

September 1964
YOU'RE HOLDING ME DOWN/ I'VE GOTTA
Coral 62492
The King Bees

A second attempt for The King Bees to make good with a John Turnbull number backed up by a John Meek song just didn't cause any interest in the group at all, they soon grew very dejected and split up tired of going nowhere.

David, who was by now calling himself Davy Jones, had met his first real manager, well *actually* a former roadie with The Moody Blues, who had come to London drawn by all of the Beatle action, and had scored with 'Go Now'. The roadie, Ralph Morten had managed to get Davy some gigs with the Manish Boys at several West End clubs, including The Marquee Club in Wardour Street, where they were second on the bill to a group The High Numbers. This gig led onto a series of six shows recorded for the Pirate radio station Radio London, where the Manish Boys again played second on the bill to The High Numbers who later became all the rage after they changed their name to The Who.

March 1965
I PITY THE FOOL/TAKE MY TIP
Parlophone R5250
David Jones & The Manish Boys
Producer: Shel Talmy
Out of the blue this single appeared and rapidly disappeared again as did the follow up.

August 1965
YOU'VE GOT A HABIT OF LEAVING/BABY LOVES IT THAT WAY
Parlophone R5315
David Jones and the Manish Boys
Producer: Shel Talmy

Well the kid was getting plenty of breaks but didn't seem to be able to pull them off!

Ralph Morten realised that it was time to call in some help, and called a Moody Blues contact, manager Ken Pitt who had already pushed The Kinks and Manfred Mann into the Charts (who were all important at the time).

'I was looking for someone who could come out of the pop world and be a star as opposed to a guitar cowboy,' recalled Pitt who thought in the established terms of 'an all round entertainer'. It was the then generally accepted fact that the'pop world' did not have stars, it had idols, and the main feature of an idol was their youth and good looks, if they had talent, then it was possible that they could become stars, if they could become all round entertainers: tap dance, tell jokes, juggle, the works, then with dedication they could become as well respected as . . . say . . . Tommy Steele, who was in fact the last of the all-round entertainers to come out of the pop world.

Pitt recognised in Davy Jones the embryo of the all-round-entertainer he was looking for one Sunday afternoon at the Marquee: 'I thought he was someone who could be groomed in just the way I had in mind,' he reminisced. 'From the way he moved on stage, by the way he held himself, and even just his eyes. Even the songs he was writing were quite remarkable.' David was playing a standard set of his singles interspersed with some of his own material which included 'Do Anything You Say', 'Good Morning Girl', 'Can't Help Thinking About Me', and 'I Say To Myself'. Pitt arranged a meeting later in Ralph's apartment in Warwick Square.

Between the three of them they put together a deal which would take Davy Jones away from his Parlophone label onto his third label in three years, Pye. This was not too unusual since the record companies were still thinking 'chart potential' and as a rule signed one year renewable contracts with new artists.

Pye put Davy Jones into the studio to record another single, by this time the companies had realised that it was often an advantage to let the artist record his own material, if it was strong enough, rather than force some tin pan alley piece-of-work onto them in the studio . . . another round of 'thank you's' are due to The Beatles for that concession . . . Pye also gave Davy a bit more help in the form of their big guns behind the mixing desk, their ace producer Tony Hatch.

The two sides of the single had been recorded when Davy got a telegram from Ken Pitt who was in New York talking to Andy Warhol about acting as his agent in the UK to represent his group Velvet Underground (with Lou Reed – store this titbit for later). While in the Big Apple, Pitt heard that Screen Gems were putting together a group of four actor/musicians whom they would call The Monkees, give them a TV series and make them overnight pop stars, unfortunately for Davy Jones, The Monkees were being fronted by an English actor called Davy Jones, Pitt reasoned that this would cause confusion and that the one in Hollywood would come out on top, so he warned Davy in time to change *his* name.

January 1966
CAN'T HELP THINKING ABOUT ME/I SAY TO MYSELF
Pye 17020 (UK)/Warner 5818 & DJ 5815 (US)
David Bowie & The Lower Third
(Dennis Taylor, Graham Rivens, Phil Lancaster)
Produced: Tony Hatch

When Pitt returned to London, David and Ralph went round to his apartment, David threw 'Oh by the way – I'm David Bowie now' into the conversation to which Pitt replied, 'That sounds a nice name.' Where the name Bowie comes from is shrouded in time-wasting conjecture; Ken Pitt always assumed that it had something to do with Bowie's mother's side of the family, but it could equally have come from the Bowie knife as the press releases claimed.

'Looking at David Bowie it would be difficult to recognise under that smart exterior the somewhat controversial and angry young singer who styled himself after his famous namesake.'

It went on to claim that David's interest in all forms of art comes from his Art School days where he studied to be a graphic designer . . . come again? Art School, graphic designer? Humm . . . 'but although I was very interested in design I found that I could not express myself satisfactorily designing graphically' . . . Thank you David Bowie! Back to reality:

Of all people around Bowie, Pitt was not taken in by the press release chirpy style and minor exaggerations, he was too long in the tooth for that; the reality of David Jones aka Bowie was that at the age of 19, already a five times flop out there in the market-place, he was still under age!

Pitt organised a post mortem with Bowie, Ralph Morten and David's parents – the result being David signing a management contract with Pitt, and exit Horton.

Pitt is a quiet, likeable, friendly man with a taste for the finer things of life; art, literature (he has a fine collection of rare books by Beardsley and Oscar Wilde). He and David had got on well from their first meeting, but Pitt was not the sort of manager who would take advantage of an up-and-coming young artist, he wanted to make sure that David knew what he was doing when signing a contract, so he brought Bowie's parents into the discussions. This was the start of a friendship between Pitt and David's father, who unlike many parents of the day, was eager to be involved in his son's career no matter how hard it got, even if it meant slipping him the odd couple of quid now and again . . . It was Mr Jones who bought Little Richard's early albums which sparked Davy off wanting to be a musician, eventually settling on jazz.

David's father and his manager often got together informally at each other's homes to discuss David's potential and direction.

Until the contracts with Ken were drawn up David had to earn a living, which meant the same for him as any other new band with or without a contract; out on the road trekking up and down the motorways to gigs in the darkest Midlands. To help them cope (and to save money on hotel bills) they bought an old ambulance which they fitted out with mattresses for overnight stops or whatever. Aside from the rough nights with The Lower Third kipping out in the ambulance, David never actually faced the realities of the struggling musician, since he still lived with his parents in Bromley and didn't have the financial hassles of paying for digs, or not paying, which others had to face. And when he signed with Pitt he moved into his manager's plush apartment's spare room in Manchester Square.

Eventually the contracts were signed in April 1966, a five year exclusive deal, by which Pitt was showing his faith in the young David Bowie.

It was clear from the start that Bowie was, in Pitt's eyes, going to be groomed for stardom and be educated about the ways of the business by Pitt, not as altogether manipulating but paternal direction. Ken Pitt is a professional manager and had learned that after the kids had lost interest in the 'teen idol' then it was onto other work or the dole queues out of the business. It was even tried with The Beatles!

But even as he was signing the contracts which would make him a runner in the race, for the first real time Bowie was looking over his shoulder at the new pop-culture he was a part of . . . some of the ten day wonders were millionaires after two years and still teen idols!

April 1966
DO ANYTHING YOU SAY/GOOD MORNING GIRL
Pye 17079
Producer: Tony Hatch

(Four of David's Pye tracks, Do Anything You Say/I Dig Everything/ Can't Help Thinking About Me/I'm Not Losing Sleep, were re-released on October, 1972, on Pye 7NX 8002 (33 ⅓ rpm).

After the flop of their first Bowie single, Pye put out their second single only four months later. There was some action happening for Bowie, he had a real manager now . . . it got nowhere despite the efforts of the press office who had forgotten about David's intellectual reasons for writing in favour of something a little closer to the truth: 'David became a full time artiste six months after leaving school'. – What, no Art School? – 'He formed a number of groups with Rhythm and Blues in mind . . . He found it easier to write his own material than to hunt for numbers'. Both sides of the single were home grown.

August 1966
I DIG EVERYTHING/I'M NOT LOSING SLEEP
Pye 17157
David Bowie
Producer: Tony Hatch

Another two Bowie songs which missed the charts, and true to record company form it was 'three-and-out', things went very quiet very suddenly at Pye for Pitt and Bowie. 'I don't really know what went wrong,' said Pitt. It seemed that Bowie was having trouble with Tony Hatch during the recording sessions, or vice versa. As quick as you could say 'blue suede shoes', Pye had slipped out of their contract and were off breathing easier for it.

For David it was back on the road again; only having gone solo for the last two singles he didn't have The Lower Third with him – but it was 1966. Out in the streets of London things were beginning to swing, Mod was the big thing. The Who were making it big with four charting singles under their belt . . . But David didn't have a band . . . but it was 1966 and Dylan had just been in town.

LOVE YOU TILL TUESDAY/ OVER THE WALL WE GO
EMI (Metal acetate disc)
David Bowie

Without a record label it was audition time and EMI passed up this song which was to resurface again a few years later.

Back on the club circuit Bowie was going solo doing a sort of double act with himself, at the Marquee he would play up the Dylanesque folk-singer side of his character dressed in black, being sincere, while still playing the all-round-entertainer bit taking his mother to gigs and ending with 'When You Walk Through A Storm'!

While he liked the idea of being an all-round-entertainer, he didn't like the Tommy Steele mould being offered to him by Ken. And so it was that as a professional manager Pitt decided that during this lull between labels, David should be broadening his performing base, well that's how it looks from here, but Pitt said of the time 'We did rather suffer at that period'.

Bowie started landing small bit parts as an actor in films, or TV, cropping up as a model occasionally.

THE IMAGE
Border Films
Michael Armstrong

Pitt said that this was a quite dreadful film, but it did bring in £30 and a little experience of film.

This experimental little piece of celluloid lasts a whole twenty minutes and features our hero as the ghost of an artist's model returned from the dead, all conveyed by silent-movie style facial close-ups showing emotion . . . gripping stuff, but not worth the £30, since part of his scene was filmed with him hanging from a window ledge one floor up while buckets of water were thrown over him to simulate rain . . . a bad deal.

During that period of suffering without a contract behind him, David began hanging out with the other young dudes on the fringe of the entertainment business, actors, singers, musicians and dancers, notably one dancer, Hermione Farthingale, he had – as they say – fallen in love.

December 1966
RUBBER BAND/LONDON BOYS
Deram DM 107 (UK)
RUBBER BAND / THERE IS A HAPPY LAND
Deram 85009 (US)
Producer: Mike Vernon

Ken Pitt had pulled off the almost impossible; a new record contract. Who would be fool enough to sign up a seven time flop! A new record company.

The Deram label had been started earlier in the year by producer Denny Cordell, and was one of the first UK independents, which realised that all you really had to do to start a record company was to get a couple of artists, enough money to record them and put out a single (this was swinging optimistic London 1966 and the pop business was boom time), then the trick was to tie in a distribution deal with a major company – Decca in the case of Deram – and go! The only other artist on the roster with David Bowie was a young Greek singer, Cat Stevens. The feeling around the halls of the London record labels ranged from scorn to a genuine belief that one of the Deram boys would make it . . . if only based on the fact that Cordell was no fool and was risking his neck.

'Rubber Band' was perhaps a little bad judgement on the part of Cordell, a jaunty little ditty about lost love with a brass band backing which wasn't right for the way the music scene was growing up.

The single's B side would probably have been a chart number. The press biog claimed that 'The London Boys' was 'David Bowie's partly autobiographical cameo of the brave and defiant little mod racing uphill along Wardour Street to an empty Paradise', a much more literate release than the others, and on second glance hints at the use of drugs . . . speed?! (If you miss it just worry about the fact that Wardour Street is flat as a pancake).

It's a social comment song sung from the inside looking around the Mod revolution seeing a young kid, every mother's son, drawn deeper into the Soho Mod drug scene of Blues and Reefers. Bowie executes the song dramatically as his voice gradually changes during the course from a well spoken and enunciated lyric into a broad cockney drawl which ends the song like a shout of triumph 'Nah yer wan uv tha Laaahndun Boyes'.

At the time wnen the drug scene was indeed penetrating the music scene and before it became almost one and the same thing, David could be said to have written the song partly from an autobiographical point of view. With the attention dope, mainly cannabis, but also Blues and Purple Hearts were getting from the press, the B side of the single would have drawn considerable attention from the fifth estate (or column), perhaps that's what Cordell was trying to avoid.

Once more, David Bowie failed to get a toehold into the bottom of the charts. But David was now being heard in the USA, or at least the single was available in the States and that counted for something even if the B side had been changed; too parochial for Americans who weren't going through Mod, or whose moralists wouldn't take kindly to drug songs coming at them from Britain when they had their hands full with that hippy stuff floating out of San Francisco!

April 1967
LAUGHING GNOME/THE GOSPEL ACCORDING TO TONY DAY
Deram DM 123 (UK)
Deram 20079 (US)
Producer: Mike Vernon

Another Bowie composition for his sins. This is an outrageously bad song about a gnome who laughs a lot and runs away 'Ha ha he, I'm the laughing gnome and you can't catch me', full of dreadful puns and Chipmunk sounds . . . it probably has some redeeming feature as a subversive

dope song for kiddies. It wasn't viewed like that (I'm making excuses). It sounds as though Bowie knuckled under and tried the all-round-entertainer type song; a cross between Tony Newley's voice and Tommy Steele's chirpiness . . . Bowie's Little White Bull . . . and ziltch!

But then on the other hand David was getting into some strange things outside the studio. He was visiting the Dance Studio regularly with his girl-friend Hermione.

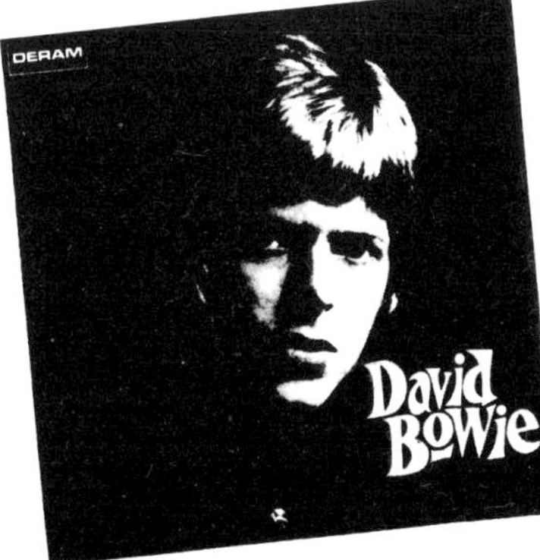

June 1967
DAVID BOWIE
Deram DML 1007
Uncle Arthur/Sell Me A Coat/Rubber Band/Love You Till Tuesday/There Is A Happy Land/We Are Hungry Men/When I Live My Dream/Little Bombardier/Silly Boy Blue/Come And Buy My Toys/Join The Gang/She's Got Medals/Maids Of Bond Street/Please Mr Gravedigger.
Producer: Mike Vernon

In America, this album was released in April 1967, as Deram 18003, but excluding We Are Hungry Men and Maids of Bond Street.

Bowie admits that he was trying to sound like Tony Newley, 'I was more Newley than Newley', he has said laughing off these days. 'Uncle Arthur' is a sort of 'She's Leaving Home' in reverse, the 32 year-old Uncle Arthur attempts to leave his mother without success. 'When I Live My Dream' could be Bowie's plea for success, sung in a sincere voice (Newley again).

Despite its obviously derivative . . . *everything*! the album has achieved cult status amongst those who go in for that sort of thing.

Over in the US – the press office were deviating from their path of truth and honesty once more 'David is memorising much of the Oxford Companion to Music . . . he adores Vaughan Williams, Dvorak, Elgar and Holst' he read a lot those days too 'He devours Camus, Pinter, Behan, Waterhouse, Rechy, and Oscar Wilde'.

The press statement said that David received congratulatory phone calls from such names to conjure with as . . . Franco Zeffirelli, Mel Tormé, Lionel Bart and Nina and Frederik (although it is not clear whether Nina & Frederik shared the call).

Didn't work! The album was a bust!

Deram pulled out the stops and threw everything they had behind the single from the album:

July 1967
LOVE YOU TILL TUESDAY/ DID YOU EVER HAVE A DREAM
Deram DM 135 (UK)/Deram 85016 (US).
Producer: Mike Vernon

Even with the promise of Ken Pitt putting up £7,000 towards a film of the same name, actually filming it, for use as a promo job the single just didn't have it, and it too was a bust! Deram had no real option but to pull out, they had wanted him to make it, attempted at least half truthful press statements, spent time and money recording an album, which few companies would have done for a new signing, Bowie just wasn't what the public wanted . . . so they too slipped out of their contract.

Deram quickly recuperated their losses with the Greek singer/songwriter, Cat Stevens, when they released his 'I Love My Dog' in October 66, followed by the smash hit No 2 'Matthew & Son'. Deram later picked up The Moody Blues and turned them into successes again with their 'Days of Future Past' album. It is interesting to compare their Bowie album with what else they were nurturing and see that they had had it all wrong – but that's with hindsight.

Ken Pitt was worried again, this time his

boy had blown his tenth chance at the top with no fewer than five labels! And that was bad news. But what was worse news was Bowie himself; he was goofing off, down Soho and Covent Garden, getting into mime instead of tap dancing, and Buddhism instead of writing songs.

This was the lowest point for David's morale, he was a failure, and was looking for something to fall into. He was already in love with Hermione, and had appeared in a short TV play as a dancing extra with her. He accompanied her everywhere, and it was at the Dance Centre where he first saw mime artist Lindsay Kemp, and the prompt which forced him backstage after the studio show was that Kemp used Bowie's Deram album as background music during the interval!

Kemp and Bowie got on well and soon David was attending Kemp's workshop classes, which he did on and off for the next two years. Kemp's credentials as a mime are impeccable; he has worked with the Ballet Rambert, Commedia Dell Arte, the Kulouki and Marcel Marceau as well as Fellini and Ken Russell. By the end of 1967 he was touring with Kemp, as part of his troupe, but never got paid. He did, however, do one Scottish TV show with Kemp for which he got £30.

So David was off broadening his artistic base, something Pitt had told him to do, but not quite in the way Pitt intended. Meanwhile a song which he had recorded as part of Ken Pitt's abortive film tie-in with the 'Love Me Till Tuesday' single, just lay in the can waiting to be turned into Bowie's first hit single.

Bowie's Buddhist phase was more disturbing than his attraction to mime. David had always claimed to have been interested in Buddhism since the age of fifteen, which is quite believable if his brother Terry had given him 'On The Road' to read. But with the commercial rejection he had gone through, religion began to hold some sort of light for him.

He had begun to reintroduce Buddhism into his life while with Deram and would frequently bring it up in interviews, but it was never made much of a feature in his press notices, since The Beatles were doing some fairly strange things to another Eastern sect in India and Bowie's trip just didn't have the newsworthiness, or Bowie didn't.

He was becoming difficult to deal with, refusing to cut his hair for an important TV show and getting kicked off. He wasn't writing and even disappeared completely for a couple of weeks to a Tibetan Buddhist monastery in the Scottish lowlands, set up by refugee monks after the invasion of Tibet by China. He was taking it all very seriously and even went as far as to consider whether to take up holy orders, cut his hair and stay in the monastery, but he decided against that one.

Returning to London he found that the 'Underground' had really hit town, dope was everywhere, the city had opened up to everything and in the forefront of the new revolution which came with the London Summer of Love (starting in 1967 and continuing till somewhere around 1969-70) were the Arts Labs.

The Arts Labs were small multi-media studios opened to free form and free thought . . . this was what David had been waiting for, he could use all of Ken Pitt's good all-round-entertainer advice in an arts lab environment.

There wasn't one in Bromley so he got one together. If this seems at odds with David's past failure as an artist, bear in mind that an Arts Lab was what you called it, and this Arts Lab was a small saloon bar room at the back of the Three Tuns pub on Beckenham High Street!

But David bummed about doing little or nothing towards his ambition of being a rock 'n' roll star. He was into his Lab and his mime troupe, Feathers, which he had formed before the Deram album but when the relationship with Hermione folded so too did the mime troupe.

As bad as things were there was still Ken Pitt behind him trying to make it work.

Going back to the dead 'Love You Till Tuesday' promo film Pitt had made, there was one song which stood apart from the rest of the shooting, it was a strange number about a spaceman floating, cut off, remote. They had filmed it as a space capsule sequence with David acting out the part of Major Tom. It is claimed by Ken that the hardened stage hands and camera crew were stunned and some were heard to hum the tune later while clearing the set . . . the one and only 'old grey whistle test', or in their case 'humming test'.

Pitt pitched in there with the film in early 1969 just as the USA was pitching in to put a man on the moon. He took the filmclip along to Philips who bought the idea and David Bowie was back in the business again.

July 1969
SPACE ODDITY/WILD EYED BOY FROM FREECLOUD
Philips 1081 (UK)/Mercury 72949 (US)
Producer: Gus Dudgeon

The single was launched with precision to ensure it caught the Americans on the moon and guaranteed current affairs interest needletime.

But despite this it only made number 48

by September 6 and it was withdrawn. But the needletime was still being given so Philips recanted and reissued and re-launched it whence it sped up to Number 5 in the UK charts before dropping out again. In all, Bowie's hit single had been in the charts for thirteen weeks.

The Moonshot was not the real influence on Bowie when he wrote the song, just the commercial hook to sell it. David credits Stanley Kubrick with the influence in the title. It departed from the US cowboy attitude to space, they were conquering space like they had conquered the West, with right and decency on their side, but Bowie's Major Tom was against that floating in his tin can high above the world, alone helpless, existential, bliss.

Very suddenly Bowie was in demand, *really* in demand, touring with big names, TV shows and the like, but David was bewildered by it all, like Major Tom, he had reached the start of what he had been working towards but he didn't know what to do with it.

RAGAZZO SOLO, RAGAZZA SOLA/ WILD EYED BOY FROM FREECLOUD
Philips 704 208 BW (Italy)

The single was doing so well that Philips Italy got David to record an Italian translation of 'Space Oddity' for their market where it too made the charts.

Philips had all they needed to put him into the studio to record his first album (for them).

November 1969
DAVID BOWIE
Philips SBL 7912 (UK)
Space Oddity/Unwashed and Somewhat Slightly Dazed/Letter To Hermione/ Cygnet Committee
Janine/An Occasional Dream/Wild Eyed Boy From Freecloud/God Knows I'm Good/ Memory Of A Free Festival
Producer: Tony Visconti/Gus Dudgeon
Musicians: David Bowie, Mick Ronson, Woody Woodmansey, Tony Visconti, Rick Wakeman, Terry Cox, Paul Buckmaster, Keith Christmas, Mick Wayne, Tim Renwick, Herbie Flowers, John Cambridge, Benny Marshall.

This album was released in the US as Man of Words, Man of Music on Mercury SR6 1216. It was re-released in October, 1972, as Space Oddity by RCA as RCA LSP 4813 (UK and US).

'Space Oddity' was obviously the show-piece cut of the album, and naturally it opens it with a different version than the single, a full five minutes in length. 'Unwashed' and 'Somewhat Slightly Dazed' is perhaps a view of Bowie's feelings as a result of the success of 'Space Oddity', but it is spoiled by Tony Visconti's over production. Following on from the screeching harmonicas of 'Unwashed' comes Bowie's love song, 'Letter To Hermione' showing just how disorientated he felt after their relation-ship collapsed. The final track on side one is Bowie's 'cry to humanity' he later said 'the Quasi-capitalist, the sponsor of the revolution puts a lot of support into the revolution and gets no thanks for it' and then there are the pure revolu-tionaries like Jerry Rubin and Abbie Hofman who put everything into the rebellion and get all the thanks, it's a magnificent, if slightly dated, track.

Side two starts with the sardonic 'Janine', which can only be viewed as a slightly schizoid song and the pre-decessor of Bowie's apparent non-sense songs which convey more image than story line. The following track is another Hermione, as tender and gently lyrical as the production. 'Wild Eyed Boy From Freecloud' is a myth maker part of the hippy dream. 'God Knows I'm Good' is almost a regression to the 'Uncle Arthur' days, while the album ends with a tribute to the sucess of the Beckenham Arts Lab free festival.

He recorded it and took off back to Bromley where, with his girlfriend, Angie, he moved into a flat in a rambling apartment block and hid out for most of the time.

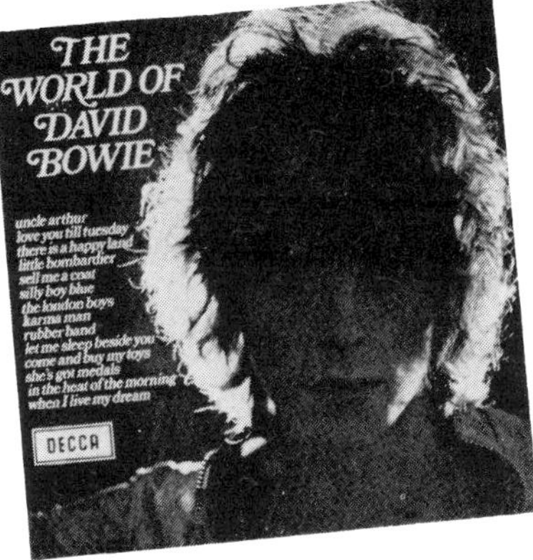

March 1970
THE WORLD OF DAVID BOWIE
Decca (S)PA58
Uncle Arthur/Love You Till Tuesday/ There Is A Happy Land/Little Bombardier/Sell Me A Coat/Silly Boy Blue/The London Boys.
Karma Man/Rubber Band/Let Me Sleep Beside You/Come And Buy My Toys/ She's Got Medals/In The Heat of the Morning/When I Live My Dream.
Producer: Mike Vernon.

This was a re-issue of Bowie's one Deram album with a few changes here and there. It was re-re-issued (!) in 1973 with a new sleeve photo to take advantage of David's Ziggy Stardust persona.

David was awarded the Ivor Novello prize for originality of songwriting by the Songwriters Guild of Great Britain, but when he ventured out to collect it he was mobbed by screaming kids – not an altogether enjoyable experience. Whenever he did play a gig it was to thousands of fans and not just the couple of hundred maximum who had turned up to see him previously. And these were 'fans' screaming, yelling, gnashing teeth and rushing the stage types. It was just too much for him.

He was totally bemused and after a short tour which took him up to Scotland, and a couple of gigs as support to Humble Pie (where he met Pete Frampton again), he wasn't into it one bit, although he did net over £1,000 for the month of October.

A quick detour over to Malta for their Song Contest, which he won (nothing like success for success), and it was back to London for a gig at the Purcell Rooms organised by a friend of his producer Tony Visconti; a Chinese American by the name of Calvin Mark Lee.

The gig was a sell-out, Ken Pitt recalls that it was probably the best gig he ever saw Bowie do, he held the audience in the palm of his hand, unfortunately none of the press turned up to give it a good review.

June 1970
PARIS STUDIO SESSION
Kooks/Queen Bitch/Song For Bob Dylan/Andy Warhol.
Musicians: David Bowie, Mick Ronson, Mick Woodmansey (Woody), Trevor Boulder, Mark Carr-Prichard, Dana Gillespie, George Underwood.

The session was more of a party than a serious recording session, George Underwood sang the song Bowie had written for him, Song For Bob Dylan and Dana Gillespie sang Andy Warhol.

DeFries was convinced that he should turn to the music business full-time and began the rounds of the record companies claiming that 'Bowie will be bigger than Dylan' – another feature of the new style management was that the accent was not upon artistic merit but on how big they could be in relation to whoever was big at the time.

June 1970
MEMORY OF A FREE FESTIVAL 2
Mercury 6052-026 (UK)/Mercury 73075 (US)
Producer: Tony Visconti.

This version of the song, which is not, despite its title, about Woodstock, but about a small free festival at the Beckenham Arts Lab, is an electrified variation on the album track with part two being an extension.

Bowie had known the Brooklyn-bred record producer Tony Visconti since 1966 when he had been brought over to the UK to produce Procul Harum's 'Whiter Shade Of Pale'. He recalls Bowie as being 'the laziest person I knew. He would sleep all day and did very little work. I was very energetic and that led to us splitting apart, because I couldn't get him to write songs or rehearse'. Visconti was living in the same flat as Bowie at the time, and it seemed that only he, David and Mick Ronson had any faith that anything good would come out of the period.

Although Bowie had had a charting single with 'Space Oddity' he had failed to take it any higher than No.5 and had failed to follow it up with anything substantial . . . he looked as though he was destined to be the classic one-hit-wonder even after 11 singles. This prospect turned him into the stereotyped, stoned-a-day hippy, afraid to try again and afraid to fail.

But Visconti hassled Bowie into the studio and offered to do more than just produce, by playing bass throughout. But the single was a flop and David retreated to his Arts Lab dejected, the past year had been both elating and depressing, compounded by the death of his father just before the release of the Big single.

Bowie was at another low ebb when he walked into the studio with Visconti with a tight schedule and only one song to fill an album.

April 1971
THE MAN WHO SOLD THE WORLD
Mercury 6338041 (UK)/Mercury 6338-041 (US).
(UK release; Jan 71); Re-released Nov 1972. RCA E-4816/A-4816
The Width Of A Circle/All The Madmen/Black Country Rock/After All Running Gun Blues/Saviour Machine/She Shook Me Cold/The Man Who Sold The World/The Supermen.
Producer: Tony Visconti.
Musicians: David Bowie, Tony Visconti, Mick Ronson, Mick Woodmansey, Ralph Mace.

This album was released in the US in November, 1970, as Mercury 61325. It was re-released by RCA in November, 1972, as RCA LSP 4816 (UK and US).

When David went into the studio with a three week deadline to record this album he only had one song written, 'Width Of A Circle', and had to write and record the lot from scratch . . . he said that it was one of the worst times of his life and that he was going through hell at the time . . . it shows, what he came out of the studio with is the first of his doom laden sexually ambiguous themes.

The album first appeared on Mercury with the 'dress cover' David reclining in a 'man's' Dress . . . quite controversial . . . actually it was a flash-back to Bowie's art school training as it's a parody of a painting by pre-Raphaelite artist Dante Gabriel Rossetti . . . but the corporate policy thought it too much for the general public . . . so in the US the cover was changed to a cartoon which totally

contradicts the content and mood and emotions pushing through the surface of the album.

The cover change angered Bowie, it was another major bone of contention pulling him further from his record company. Later when RCA got hold of the rights to the album they changed the cover yet again . . . to the familiar high stepping Bowie circa Ziggy Stardust.

Bowie's existential feelings were gradually overtaken by Nietzchean solutions in his writing, Major Tom's floating above the world with nothing he could do had become terror and paranoia as the world seemed to be advancing towards doom; 'Running Gun Blues' sets the scene, while 'The Man

Who Sold The World' isn't quite the good guy he should be, given his achievement . . . there's something dark and ominous about him – which is best shown by Lulu's version of the song which Bowie arranged for her – Who is he? Hitler? Christ? Or some sort of Superman? The answer is never given directly, perhaps 'The Supermen' is some sort of answer.

This pseudo-prophetic theme starts with 'The Man Who Sold The World' and runs through most of his forthcoming albums: 'Five Years', on 'Ziggy Stardust', 'Aladdin Sane', 'Diamond Dogs' etc all started here.

This was to be the last Bowie-Visconti collaboration for four years as Visconti had teamed up with Marc Bolan and felt that Bolan was more interested in making records, unlike Bowie, and as a a professional producer, he had to move on.

This was to be the last of his Philips/ Mercury recordings as he sank deeper and deeper into hibernation in Bromley to wait for the release of the album.

Down in Bromley he had built a social set for himself which included many minor names and a few major figures in the business, such as Marc Bolan and Tony Visconti who actually had a flat in the same rambling apartment block as Bowie.

Increasingly they became his pre-occupation and Ken Pitt, the manager and friend, ceased to play a major role in David's life, while David himself was going through changes brought on by his contact with other creative people of his own age group, and of course there was always Angie.

David and Angie met at a music industry gig ostensibly to push Island Records' new heavy synth-rock band King Crimson, but it degenerated into a righteous drinking party. David had been invited by the management agency Chrysalis (later to blossom as Chrysalis Records), who held a portion of David's publishing rights, while Angie had been brought by Lou Reizner. They sat next to each other and wham bam, that was it.

Being an American, Angie started getting letters from the Home Office warning her that her work permit was soon to run out and so David and Angie got married on March 20, 1970.
Ken Pitt wasn't invited or told of the happy event, in George Tremlett's Biography of Bowie Pitt expresses his disappointment over this, but he shouldn't have, David's mother wasn't invited either and she only heard of it at the last minute.

Bowie's set was widened through Visconti to include Marc Bolan, Rick Wakeman and various sessions musicians which pulled him further away from Pitt, and place him further out of Pitt's ideal of what was required in the business, a belief which by this time had become outmoded and untrue.

December 1970
ALL THE MADMEN/ALL THE MADMEN (2)
Mercury 73173 (US).

In December Mercury released the above single and called David over to promote it, but there was a screw-up over his work permit and he couldn't perform. This US visit was a failure, to say the least, being dragged around radio stations with the single and 'The Man Who Sold The World' album, without any gigs to support the sales, no wonder it became known as the 'Secret American Tour'.

He did manage a few clandestine performances though, mostly free gigs with him solo with his guitar . . . songs from the album without backing to add the atmosphere . . . being forced to sell himself short.

An indication of the strength of his feelings about the change of album cover was given when he performed at the Quiet Night in Chicago in the infamous dress. Things were coming to a head with Mercury.

While in the States he took up Ken Pitt's introduction to the Andy Warhol circus at the Factory where he be-friended Lou Reed (of the Velvet Underground) who was on the verge of breaking free of the Velvets for a solo career, and they hung out around Max's Kansas City the New York centre of the decadent seventies.

On his return from the US Bowie was more determined to pursue his own concept of stardom and leave Pitt's views behind him. He explored various ideas including forming a group with Marc Bolan.

Bolan had been in the business as long as Bowie but with more success, he had been with a group, John's Children during the early hippy period (1966) before breaking away as part of a duet in 1968 firstly known as Tyrannosaurus Rex which created myths and legends which fit into the hippy consciousness backed by a soft-acid-rock which was known as 'progressive' or 'underground'. The fringe interest in progressive music exploded in late 1970 with the release of Bolan's 'Ride A White Swan' with the abbreviated band name T. Rex, which led onto a string of hit singles.

It was between Bolan's progressive

phase ending and the chart success that he and Bowie got together in the studio to record:

March 1970
THE PRETTIEST STAR/ CONVERSATION PIECE
Mercury 1135 (UK)
Producer: Tony Visconti;
Musicians: The Hype (David Bowie, Marc Bolan, Mick Ronson, Woody Woodmansey and possibly Rick Wakeman).

Another flop single which was rapidly withdrawn and lost forever. The A side reappears on 'Aladdin Sane' without Bolan and a shadow of its former glory.

Bolan had a unique deal going for himself; he was his own manager, publisher and agent and was able to give David valuable advice on how to conduct his affairs . . . starting with getting rid of Mr Ten Percent Pitt.

Bowie was introduced to Olaf Wyper, the man who had brought the Sun Label catalogue to Phonogram/Philips UK from the US, and it was Wyper who suggested that David start to get out of his contract with Ken Pitt, since Bowie felt that Pitt was holding back his career by trying to force him into the Tony Newley straitjacket. For this he needed a lawyer, Wyper passed Bowie on to his own lawyer who was gathering a name for himself around London as a man who was good at getting people out of contracts they didn't want to be in . . . the lawyer was Tony DeFries . . . this contradicts Ken Pitt's view of what happened, blaming the introduction of Bowie to DeFries on Tony Visconti of whom Pitt said 'Tony was the typical New York draft-dodging-anarchist. He used to put down all agents and managers', this may be true and Visconti may well have been all of these things in Pitt's eyes, but he did not push David towards DeFries.

DeFries was a sharp young lawyer from Shepherd's Bush who had come into the music scene through that particularly grey area where music and fashion mix. He had represented models in the late sixties and led an abortive attempt to form a fashion model union and by the time Bowie happened along to his office he had rightly acquired a reputation as a contractual wizard. He looked over David's contracts with Pitt and decided that he could in fact help: 'I felt sorry for Bowie,' he said a few years later in an interview with Melody Maker. 'I thought "Poor little chap he's got himself into a terrible mess",' and started the moves to get the contract overturned. The first problem to overcome was the two years left to run on the contract. It was suggested that Bowie (and DeFries) buy Pitt out for £2,000 but for some reason they didn't want to. Eventually DeFries convinced all those involved that it would be a good idea if all of the terms of the contract were forgotten . . . and they were.

This left Bowie without a manager, he turned to DeFries, 'The next thing I knew was that he had brought Angie with him to see me,' said DeFries, 'which is David's way of showing faith,' and they signed contracts.

Bowie commented to George Tremlett at the time about Pitt, 'He is a very nice man, I like him very much – but that's not enough in this business.' He was right, the business was changing from a managerial point of view. The old style managers with artistic vision (right or wrong) were being left behind by the fast young lawyer managers who not only knew their way around the business but could walk in or out of contracts at will, or make things so difficult for those with whom they were dealing that life was impossible. Allen Klein and Tony DeFries were of this mould.

The first stage in Bowie's new career was to get him a new recording contract with yet another record company, and to develop an image which will not only catch the public eye but ensure front page coverage in the press.

In order to do this DeFries had to have more than just a passing knowledge of Bowie's work. To this end he spent several months listening to David's past material, good and bad, and attended a session at the Paris Studio.

January 1971
HOLY HOLY/BLACK COUNTRY ROCK
Mercury 6052-049 (UK).
Producers: Blue Mink/Tony Visconti.
Musicians: David Bowie, Mick Ronson, Tony Visconti, Ralph Mace, Herbie Flowers, Mick Woodmansey.

An abortive single which bombed out in the charts. David later re-cut it on the flip-side of the 'Diamond Dogs' single in May 1974.

1971
ZIGGY 2
Queen Bitch/Bombers/Supermen/ Looking For A Friend/Almost Grown/ Kooks/Song For Bob Dylan/Andy Warhol/It Ain't Easy/It's Going To Be Me
Musicians: Bowie, Mark Pritchard,

Mick Ronson, Woody Woodmansey, Trevor Boulder, Jeff Alexander, George Underwood, Dana Gillespie, Marc Bolan.

There were two main contenders for the new-improved Bowie; RCA and CBS, but the latter dropped out of the running despite liking the acetate of the product Bowie and DeFries would bring to the label, Clive Davis, president of Columbia in New York, had been put off by David's sexually ambivalent Lauren Bacall looks.

'Besides DeFries was asking a lot,' said Dan Loggins, head of A&R at CBS London; 'Bowie had just come off two loser albums for Mercury.'

DeFries was left with RCA, who were on the up-swing after a rather depressing decade during the sixties where they only had Jefferson Airplane and Elvis Presley.

The forerunners at RCA who were shaping the new policy for the seventies were Bob Ringe and Dennis Katz. It was Katz who had been totally bowled over with the acetate DeFries had brought along and who eventually affixed his name to the contract; soon Katz was echoing DeFries' statements about Bowie. 'I think potentially he's as big as Presley'; this did not mean that Bowie was as big as Presley at the time, just that he may be. Also note the subtle change between DeFries' statement and Katz's 'Dylan' was changed to 'Presley' – Dylan was on CBS; Presley on RCA!

Things were going well for Bowie once more, a new manager and a new record deal.

ZIGGY PLAYED GUITAR

Confident with the new deal Bowie began coming out of his semi-seclusion in Bromley. DeFries and RCA had lined up interviews with the music press and David was revelling in them and was already anticipating his success by 'discovering' other new artists whom he was going to produce and lead to stardom: Arnold Corns was one and Rudi Valentino was another, both were students at Dulwich College at the time but David would lead them on to other things through one of his compositions: 'Moonage Daydream' which would be backed by 'Hang Onto Yourself', another Bowie composition.

DeFries was pushing David towards fulfilling what David believed the public wanted; a superstar. Someone who could do the outrageous and get away with it (the dress was an example). Bowie wanted to be a superstar so he'd better act like one . . . out came the black limos and chauffeurs, press conferences in London's top hotels (afterwards the limo would take David back to Bromley to wife and son and domestic bliss).

It would be too glib to say that the music industry was waiting for David Bowie, or to say that the David Bowie who emerged from the RCA offices was a carefully pre-fabricated star, or that Bowie was controlling the media perfectly. There have been so many 'instant' stars the industry (and the public) couldn't have been waiting for them all at once. As for pre-fabrication, Bowie had been developing his personality within the music scene for almost eight years and it was a difficult process of trial and error (mostly error). It is also difficult to see how someone, who couldn't control himself in concert without the paranoia Bowie had felt following the success of 'Space Oddity, could control the media. But all of these factors came together to create a STAR.

The turn of the decade had been a disappointing anti-climax to the smoking stoned days of the late sixties; most of the barriers had been pulled down during the days of peace acid electric love, there were no new frontiers to be crossed . . . well only one; homosexuality which had only recently been legalised.

The early seventies saw Glam Rock (a generic term) which drew all forms of camp under a rather derogatory umbrella; T Rex with Marc Bolan's glittered cheeks, Sweet in their silver suits and somewhat dubious lipstick, and Gary Glitter romped through the charts playing totally different styles of music, but because of their similar stage appearances they all were part of Glam Rock. From America came Lou Reed with his black eyeshadow and valium, and Alice Cooper (a man who called himself Alice, an actor who had been turned into a rock star and who treated the rock stage as a venue for a dramatic performance in which he disembowelled dolls and executed himself by artful means two shows a night). This wasn't rock 'n' roll, this was . . . er . . . genocide?

So it was that after a year of almost

total seclusion David Bowie hit the scene (forget the first eight years, they were just stepping-stones). When giving interviews he dressed UP (as opposed to down) as though he was going on stage, interviewers quoted his hair as being light brown (natural), or blond, or orange, or any colour he decided to dye it that week. Off stage this guy was sensational and the press looking for a real star were quick to grab as much lineage out of him as possible.

And so when the RCA album was released the press grabbed it with glee:

December 1971
HUNKY DORY
RCA SF 8244 (UK)/RCA LSP 4623 (US).
Changes/Oh, You Pretty Things/Eight Line Poem/Life On Mars/Kooks/ Quicksand.
Fill Your Heart/Andy Warhol/ Song For Bob Dylan/Queen Bitch/ The Bewlay Brothers.
Producer: Ken Scott.

This is Bowie's most optimistic album, the title Hunky Dory, is Cockney slang for 'OK' or 'everything's good', an indication of the feelings surrounding a big contract with an international company which sells records.

Starting with 'Changes', an up-tempo rocking number containing the view of his past career 'every time I thought I'd got it made, it seemed the taste was not so sweet', then he widens the song to take in the unrest he found in the US over Vietnam and the way the country was going. He takes this further in 'Oh! You Pretty Things' with his view that the 'youth culture' is the vanguard of a different sort of human: Homo Superior, who will take over . . . a mixture of Nietzchean philosophy and popular hippy new instant mythology.

There's a little of the old pain in 'Eight Line Poem', followed by the return to the main theme, the cut-up images of America's tortured brow with the plea; 'Life On Mars?'

'Kooks' provides a brief interlude showing, as Bowie later said, 'how slushy and sentimental a songwriter can get', written for his son Zowie while listening to Neil Young – a romantic little ditty.

'Quicksand' takes us back to the 'other worldly' combination of surrealism and existentialism 'knowledge comes with death's release' and then swings into the homo superior aspirations taking Side A to a conclusion on a down note.

Side B starts optimistically enough with 'Fill Your Heart', a song about spiritual freedom (hippy style); 'gentleness will cleanse your soul'. 'Andy Warhol' is another step out of the theme, but not quite so far as 'Kooks', about Warhol and his circus, introducing the decadent scene which reappears later.

The plea to Bob Dylan to come back to the 'Revolution' with a couple of songs from his old scrapbook starts in a similar way as Dylan's own 'Song For Woody' (Guthrie) which goes 'Hey Woody Guthrie I wrote you a song'.

Decadence returns with all of the bi-sexuality of 'Queen Bitch', which is reminiscent of The Velvet Underground's 'White Light White Heat', remember; the Velvets were being produced by Andy Warhol and were a part of his peculiar circus.

'The Bewlay Brothers' is Bowie's tour de force on the album, allusions to his changes come in odd surrealistic lines, 'we wore the clothes' and the 'dress is hung' and drugs with the exultant 'We were so turned on'. Bowie later explained that it was written about himself and his brother, Terry, but sometimes it's best not to look at the reality of the inspiration but the strange visions which songs plant . . . and this one plants so many.

There are several songs which didn't make it onto the album, and were supposed to be on a follow-up LP featuring: He's A Goldmine/Bombers/ Star Man/Round And Round/Something.

It didn't appear, but isolated tracks have surfaced.

Following the release of Hunky Dory, RCA set up a gig in Aylesbury Town Hall where Bowie shared the bill with Iggy Pop, and flew in at least $25,000 worth of US journalists to review the gig sitting on the floor. One of them, not unnaturally was a scribe from Andy Warhol's Interview magazine who observed that the show started with

Beethoven's 'Song To Joy' to herald the entry of a new-style Bowie: Orange hair and strange clothes . . . and Ziggy Stardust played guitar. It was Ziggy. Amongst the Hunky Dory numbers came songs about a rock 'n' roll hero nobody had heard of: Ziggy Stardust/Star Man/Hang Onto Yourself/Moonage Daydream/Suffragette City/Rock 'n' Roll Suicide as well as two Velvets' numbers 'White Light White Heat' and ending the concert with 'Waiting For The Man'.

The Bowie who went out on tour was a different David Bowie to any other which had been seen in the past; no coy Tony Newley, no trendy young mod, no suffering artist, but a high stepping strutting Star.

January 1972
CHANGES/ANDY WARHOL
RCA 2160 (UK) RCA 74 0605 (US)

The single from the album didn't actually make the charts, but drew a lot of attention towards this new sensational star. If he was to be the next big thing, others wanted a piece of the action, and Bowie was press-ganged into the studio to help Mickey Most resurrect the career of ex Herman's Hermits' front man, Peter Noone.

May 1972
Peter Noone
OH YOU PRETTY THINGS
RAK 114.

The single, with Bowie on piano, charted at number 12 on May 22, where it stayed for twelve weeks, and while it helped, was no more than the last, dying cough of Noone's career.

Out on the road Bowie was gathering press quotes of the order of, 'he behaves like a Soho stripper on stage', or quotes from his own mouth. 'I think it's shocking,' talking about his shaved eyebrows. 'It's a lot to do with vanity and making people look twice' . . . one description of him from The Daily Express, Jean Rook, (the woman writer men *can't* ignore!) ran: 'The pop star with the poison green eyelids and the hair like an orange lavatory brush' . . . good or bad copy Bowie was news . . . in the time honoured tradition which took The Beatles to the top, the press followed him with their notebooks (the music press with their cassette recorders).

The BIG story broke when Michael Watts of Melody Maker asked about a statement David had made in the US (on the secret tour). When asked at an LA party about his publicity he replied: 'Tell them they can make up their minds about me when I begin to get adverse publicity; when I'm found in bed with Raquel Welch's husband' . . .

It was very suddenly time to pull out all the stops. 'I'm gay,' Bowie told Michael Watts and there it was splashed all across MM's front cover OH YOU PRETTY THING . . . the shit really hit the fans then.

The Daily Express wanted interviews and, when they got them, came away with stories like: David is a self-confessed bisexual "I'm not embarrassed about it. Are you?" he asks. The answer, inevitably is 'yes' . . . that's about par for the Express (self-confessed is a ploy journalists use when someone *admits* to something *their* paper disapproves of usually used thus: A self-confessed killer – etc. yawn).

The songs for Ziggy Stardust had already been written and most recorded in the time honoured tradition in the record business that the second album must be released to catch the wave of publicity following the first, and Bowie was no exception. RCA had pulled out the big guns and were hyping him hard with a series of gigs in Southern England and an appearance on John Peel's 'underground programme' Top Gear, on national radio where Bowie unveiled Ziggy Stardust/Moonage Daydream/Hang Onto Yourself/White Light White Heat.

The concerts continued culminating in two London gigs, one at the Festival Hall where Lou Reed and the Velvets were on the bill making it an all RCA night, and another at the Finsbury Park Rainbow where Bowie called upon his ex-mentor Lindsay Kemp and his troupe to perform.

And then it was time for new product:

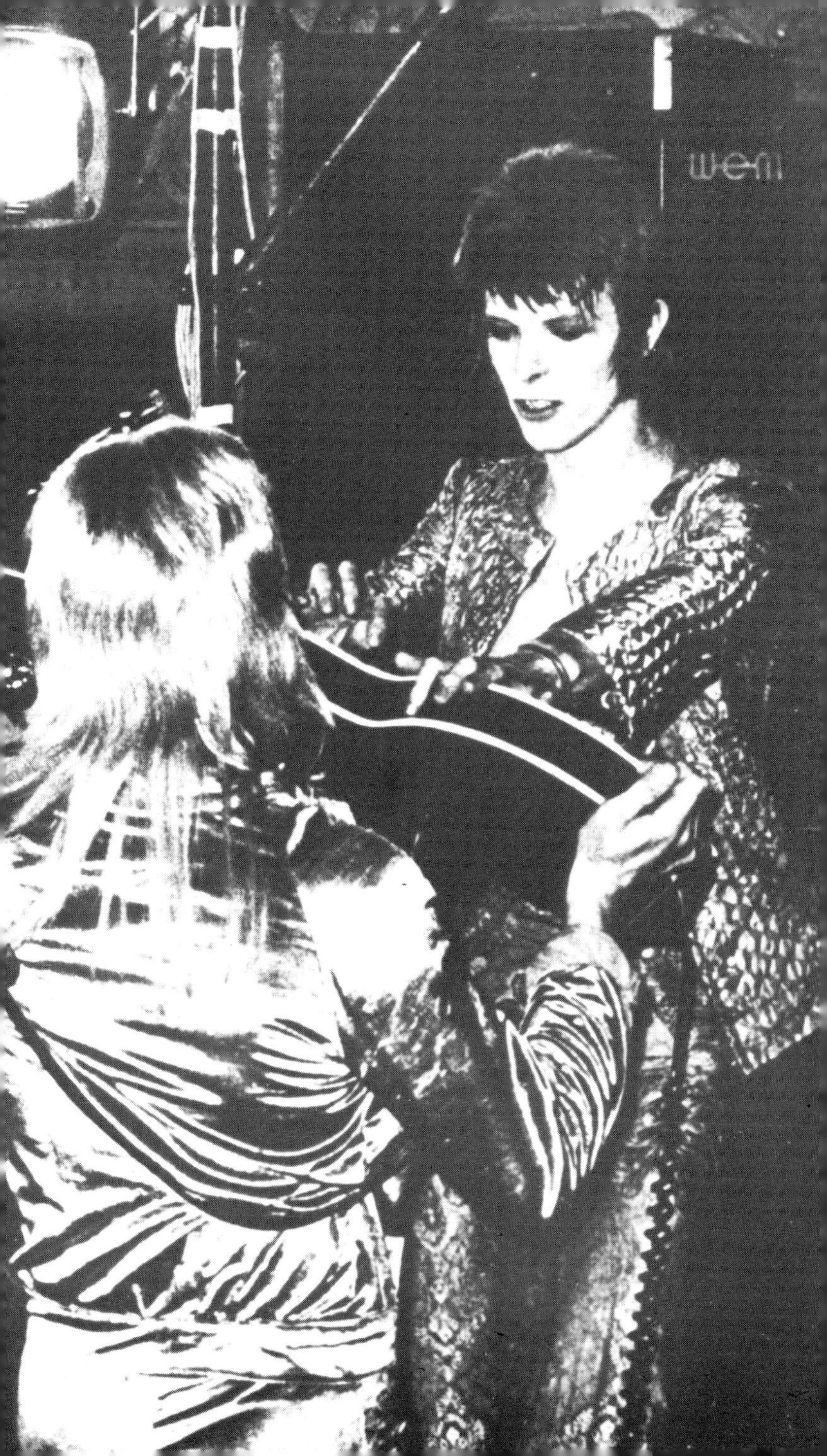
wem

June 1972
THE RISE AND FALL OF ZIGGY STARDUST AND THE SPIDERS FROM MARS
RCA SF8287 (UK)/RCA LSP 4702 (US).
American release delayed until October.
Five Years/Soul Love/Moonage Daydream/Starman/It Ain't Easy.
Lady Stardust/Star/Hang On To Yourself/Ziggy Stardust/Suffragette City/Rock 'n' Roll Suicide.
Producers: Ken Scott/David Bowie.

Bowie's follow-up album to Hunky Dory followed the concept of the Beatles' Sgt. Peppers Lonely Hearts Club Band, in that it featured a mythical musician, in Bowie's case, a space-age rock star, written before he became a star himself. David had apparently written the thing around the combination of a TV western, where an old C&W singer was booed off stage, and a story about Vince Taylor who took his rock adulation too far and proclaimed himself Christ on stage.

The first side sets the scene; the Earth is dying (sounds familiar?), 'Five Years' lays it all out with images of America, ice-cream parlours. As the newsman cries on TV the madness and decay of the West fade as the girl with the milk shake smiles and waves, but the song degenerates into the 'Five Years' scream of panic . . . As an aside, the chant of the Youth For Nixon, 1972 being election year in the US, was 'four more years' irrelevant?

'Soul Love' brings the chaos into religious context, sung in a cockney voice, with man's capacity for love in the face of doom, but God loves too . . . Rock power chords herald the entry of the new messiah, the Alligator, the Space invader, who offers the way out in a 'Moonage Daydream', sort of cosmic acid trip with all of the Sci-fi trappings; the ray guns and electric eyes of the new technology as he gathers his people. A flashback to the early days of Stardust, is given with 'Lady Stardust' who sang all night . . . the sex of Lady Stardust is confused with contradictions. 'Lady' Stardust wore make-up but he was all right.

'It Ain't Easy' is Stardust's song of Doom and salvation . . . the temptation of Christ? With a vaguely Jagger voice the answer is clear; give the woman what she wants, and the Lord will take care of you.

Ziggy's calling, the 'Starman' cuts into his radio with instructions, 'let the children boogie', confirmation by phone to a friend 'Hey that's far-out so you heard him too'. As a Rock 'n' Roll *Star* he could make it all worthwhile and even fall asleep – anyway he could do with the money.

The perks of a Rock-messiah become clear in 'Hang Onto Yourself', dispensing love amongst his followers, balling like tigers on vaseline.

'Ziggy Stardust' rode to the top and further, with weird and Gilly and the Spiders from Mars, playing left-hand with screwed up eyes and screwed down hair, like Hendrix who had died in August 1970. Both Ziggy and Hendrix took it all too far, hints of voodoo and making love to their guitars make the comparison complete. But there the comparison ended, Ziggy was a white-man surrounded by the trappings of space mythical tech.

'Suffragette City' is pure rock-star sex, raunchy, back breaking with trans-atlantic phone-calls. Ziggy's end came abruptly, a 'Rock 'n' Roll Suicide' with a breakdown and the withdrawal into himself while his friends try to inject hope into the dying star. No you're not alone, but Ziggy had played the messiah to the end.

Released while on tour in the UK, 'Ziggy Stardust' hit the public and the critics at the right time, they were looking for a new superstar, and Bowie fitted the bill, his songs were about the star-trip and not homely little boy-girl love stories.

MY RADIO SWEETHEART
Crash Records.
Ziggy Stardust/Waiting For The Man/The Supermen/Queen Bitch/Suffragette City.
White Light White Heat/Hang Onto Yourself (1)/Hang Onto Yourself (2)/Moonage Daydream/Watch That Man.
Side A comes from 'The Sound of The Seventies' BBC radio show in late 1972, as do the first two tracks on Side B. The remaining tracks are from the Long Beach concert of March 10, 1973.

On the stage the man played it like a star, which he wasn't – strictly speaking – dressed like Ziggy with make-up and bright orange hair he played it for real. Ziggy was his creation and he was becoming more and more like the messiah figure he had created . . . hell his band were even called The Spiders from Mars, and *they* were Ziggy's band. In the audiences the kids were already emulating their hero, with their orange feathered hair they hung onto every word.

Ziggy took his message back to where he said it has been conceived; America. In September he arrived in New York, the journalist's junket in May had paid off: he rated copy in Time and Newsweek.

The first gig at Carnegie Hall had attracted a gaggle of rock names; Albert Grossman, Andy Warhol etc. and a collection of advance Ziggy clones who were expecting a sort of British Alice Cooper; glam-rock being glam-rock being glam-rock . . . but they got the full Ziggy Stardust story complete with Ziggy going down on Mick Ronson's guitar, pure rock 'n' roll with none of the the theatrics of Cooper's baby disembowelling.

Eight gigs after his opening in New York, Ziggy was in Santa Monica at the Civic Auditorium playing the full range of Ziggy/Bowie numbers from 'Space Oddity' to 'Rock 'n' Roll Suicide' to a packed amphitheatre and god knows how many people out in radioland:

April 1972
STARMAN/SUFFRAGETTE CITY
RCA 2199 (UK)/RCA 74 0719 (US).
Producers: Ken Scott/David Bowie.

It shot up the charts in the UK without Bowie's help, but with the help of the hordes of Bowie-Ziggy look-alikes. Ziggy was hot property in the UK with a strong gang following as they took his identification with Ziggy to the limit. They took his message too far, and it became violent, it happened to coincide with Clockwork Orange, the science-fiction street violence of a decaying society . . . Ziggy fitted in with that . . . he came onstage to the Clockwork theme (*The Ninth Symphony* . . . Beethoven). He was the messiah; spray paint slogans on the walls proclaimed 'BOWIE IS ZIGGY ZIGGY IS GOD' . . . but Ziggy's hippie love-will-save-us became scarred with violence as his following spread and was taken up by the young gangs and Ziggy became not the messiah but the fascist anti-Christ . . . just as Bowie had predicted, 'When the kids had killed the man I had to break up the band'.

September 1972
JOHN I'M ONLY DANCING/ HANG ONTO YOURSELF
RCA 2263 (UK)/Germany & Holland 74-16216.
Producers: David Bowie (A Side)/ Ken Scott, David Bowie (B Side).
David Bowie & The Spiders From Mars.

There are several versions of the A side of this single; the original, released in 1972, is the Changes One – Bowie version with acoustic guitar. Another version, recorded during the Aladdin Sane sessions has a more punchy sound with a backing sax, this is the version which has become the standard, while a third, soul attempt was recorded during the Young American Sessions at Sigma Sound in 1974 but was left in the can.

As soon as Starman had begun to drop from the charts RCA followed it up with this single but withdrew it in favour of:

October 1972
IN PERSON
Trademark of Quality.
TMQ 71062/TMQ 71054.
Hang Onto Yourself/Ziggy Stardust/ Changes/Supermen/Life On Mars/ Five Years.
Space Oddity/Andy Warhol/My Death/ Suffragette City/John I'm Only Dancing/ Rock 'n' Roll Suicide/Width Of A Circle/ Queen Bitch/Moonage Daydream.
Recorded from FM radio (the quality of the original album is very good) during the 1972 US tour when Bowie split his set and played the second half as an acoustic part with Mick Ronson backing him on bass. The non-Bowie track, 'My Death', was written by the late Jacques Brel, the Belgian surrealist songwriter.

Bowie was introducing himself and the band as Ziggy Stardust and The Spiders From Mars. By this time, the character had become a Frankenstein monster as he lived out the Prophecy.

November 1972
THE JEAN GENIE/ZIGGY STARDUST
RCA 2302 (UK)/16238 (Germany)
THE JEAN GENIE/HANG ONTO YOURSELF
RCA 0838 (US & Italy)/41057 (France).
Producers: David Bowie (A Side)/ Ken Scott, David Bowie (B Side).

This was a much better attempt at a

chart follow-up and an advance taster for the Aladdin Sane album, some of which had already been written and recorded – he unveiled 'Drive In Saturday' in Miami in mid November by fitting it right into the Ziggy story: 'It's the year 2033 and people had to learn how to make love again by watching video films'. But for some reason he didn't play the single, with all of its overt homosexuality.

By the end of November he was in Pittsburgh and took a cab over to Philadelphia to jam onstage with Mott The Hoople on 'All The Young Dudes' which Bowie had given to Mott The Hoople earlier in the year.

September 1972
ALL THE YOUNG DUDES
CBS 8271/45673-45.
Bowie had helped save the band which was breaking up by offering them 'Suffragette City', but because of their problems at the time they couldn't record it. Bowie took them along to Tony DeFries where they became a Mainman act after DeFries had sorted out their debts. A contract with CBS followed and Bowie had helped them cut the above album and single by arranging the strings section, playing sax and adding back-up vocals with Mick Ronson.

In November RCA re-released David's two Philips albums 'David Bowie' (which was re-titled 'Space Oddity' – RCA LSP 4813) and 'The Man Who Sold The World' (RCA LSP 4816). Identical catalogue numbers were used in America.

Bowie's big year, 1972, was at an end . . . he had triumphed and broken America, the ten years of messing about had paid off with the release of two albums, three if you count the re-issue of The Man Who Sold The World, there were four 'hit' singles and a bomber, and he had completed a 13 gig US tour as well as finding the time to work out on four other projects:

HANG ONTO YOURSELF/
MAN IN THE MIDDLE
Arnold Corns (Spiders from Mars).
B&C CB 189 (US, re-issued Mooncrest 25).

The single which was really Bowie and the Spiders was recorded to allow something else to come out with Bowie on it, but without the pressures of having his name attached . . . it failed and the Spiders reverted to being The Spiders.

RAW POWER
Iggy Pop.
Columbia CBS 65586 (Re-released May 1977 as Embassy 31464).

Iggy had been a part of the Detroit scene transplanted in New York with Andy Warhol and the Velvets. He got Bowie to produce the above album but the two fell out when press-time came around and Iggy started badmouthing his producer over what a bad job he had done on the album.

TRANSFORMER
Lou Reed.
RCA LSP 4807.
Satellite Of Love.

Having encountered Lou Reed on several visits to New York, David sealed their friendship by producing this album along with Mick Ronson. He also added backing vocals throughout. Transformer activated a renaissance for Reed both commercially and artistically: 'Walk On The Wild Side', the album's best track, became a hit single and, ultimately, Reed's best known work.

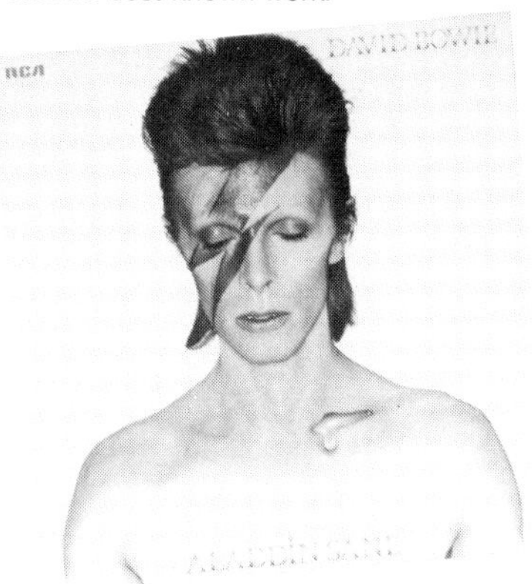

April 1973
ALADDIN SANE
RCA 1001 (UK)/RCA LSP 4852 (US).
Watch That Man/Aladdin Sane/Drive-In Saturday/Panic In Detroit/Cracked Actor. Time/The Prettiest Star/Let's Spend The Night Together/Jean Genie/Lady Grinning Soul.
Producers: Ken Scott/David Bowie.

After a short break it was back into the studio to record a new album; 'A Lad In Vein', which was tempered down to 'A Land Insane' and ultimately by a process of repetition became 'Aladdin Sane'.

A horrific transformation of Ziggy Stardust as he journeyed across

America (Bowie's rail tour in Autumn of the previous year). The whole Ziggy Stardust machine had become oppressive to Bowie; the kids in the stalls were turning out dressed as their hero, Ziggy, who had no real relationship to Bowie except that Ziggy was created out of his imagination . . . 'People were treating me as they would have treated Ziggy . . . I was the NEXT BIG THING . . . I became convinced that I was the next messiah' he said in an interview in the late seventies . . . 'But remember that at the time I was very young and full of life, it all seemed as though I was making a very positive artistic statement. I thought that it was a beautiful piece of art . . . but the fucker wouldn't leave me alone and that's when it all started going bad and I started taking Ziggy into interviews'.

Aladdin Sane was an attempt to put his experiences of the US tour onto disc, a sort of exorcism of the demon. The title track juxtaposes the images of the pretty things of the 'new elite' snorting their cocaine and drinking champagne immediately before the battlecries ring out calling them to destruction (just as they did in 1913 and 1938, and were doing at the time, since Vietnam was still uppermost in the minds and TV's of the world).

The Supermen of Ziggy's set had faded into the half-dark past and the children had lost the ability to love. 'Drive-In Saturday' shows a scene of loneliness where the youths have to go to the drive-in movies to be shown how to make love (as opposed to going to the drive-in to make love).

'Cracked Actor' came out of David's Hollywood Visit where he saw the decadence of the babylon city where the ostensibly straight heroes of the silver screen were running around making out with teenage teeny-boppers and doing all manner of white powders.

The association with Iggy Pop and the Raw Power album showed Bowie the way into two songs, 'Jean Genie', and 'Panic In Detroit'. 'Jean Genie', commonly thought to be about Jean Genet, the French author widely known for his homosexual leanings ('lives on his back . . . loves chimney stacks') is nothing of the sort, it's about Iggy . . . similar sort of thing without the literary illusions, and of course there's the Genie in the Aladdin story who comes out of the lantern in a puff of smoke.

The other Iggy inspired track, 'Panic In Detroit', is about the violence of the Motor City, which was enjoying a R 'n' R boom with bands coming out like MC5, Suzy Quatro and The Detroit Spinners (Detroit Spinners!?) a very heavy industrial sound (for the most part) which Bowie managed to capture in the song, he fed in the political growth of the White Panther party (who became in the song the National People's Gang) and Che Guevara (played by the manly Iggy Pop).

'Time' starts side two off on a low degrading note, written in New Orleans it has an underworld Euro-feel about it, it's quite easy to feel Time flexing like a whore . . . although I'm not too sure about the next line, the seriousness of the song is realised when it is understood that when time demands Billy Dolls and other friends of mine Bowie is talking about Billy Murcia, of the New York Dolls, who died when Bowie was in the US.

Passing on quickly to 'Let's Spend The Night Together', Bowie adds a whole new dimension to the Jagger/Richards song not only in his treatment of the actual piece but in the addition of the by now famous voice over declaration of explicit love with which he ends . . . Let's Make Love . . . yea why not?

April 1973
DRIVE IN SATURDAY/ ROUND AND ROUND
RCA 2353 (UK).

The flip side of this single has a legend attached; it is thought in some quarters to have been cut for inclusion on the Ziggy Stardust album and dropped in favour of Starman. Who knows? However, if it is true, as early pre-release master tapes show it in Starman's place it would have messed up the theme running through the album . . . my feeling is that whoever made the choice, Bowie – I assume, got it right at the last moment . . . a Chuck Berry number has no place on that particular platter!

Other tracks recorded for possible inclusion on the album but didn't actually make it are: All The Young Dudes/ Round And Round (studio version)/ Holy Holy (reworking)/John I'm Only Dancing (with horn section)/Instrumental (like Sweet Thing).

Without waiting for the release of the new album Bowie was back on the road starting in New York on St Valentine's Day:

February 1973
ST VALENTINE'S DAY
Radio City Music Hall NY.
Intro (Clockwork Orange theme)/Hang Onto Yourself/Ziggy Stardust/Changes/ Soul Love/John I'm Only Dancing/ Moonage Daydream/Five Years/

Space Oddity/My Death/Watch That Man/ Drive In Saturday/Aladdin Sane/Panic In Detroit/Cracked Actor/Width Of A Circle/ Time/Prettiest Star/Let's Spend The Night Together/Jean Genie/Suffragette City/Rock 'n' Roll Suicide.

Descending to the stage from the roof of the hall Bowie amazed the audience with the tightness of the set and the number of costume changes and the backdrop film of the cosmos spinning towards the audience at breathtaking speed.

The show seemed to go on forever culminating in Rock 'n' Roll Suicide with Bowie collapsing at the end as a tape fired gunshots at him; the audience were on their feet with a mixture of horror (the split second fear that Bowie/ Ziggy might have been the victim of his own predictions and become the martyr), such was the persuasive excellence of the gig.

June 1973
LIFE ON MARS/THE MAN WHO SOLD THE WORLD
RCA 2316 (UK).
TIME/PRETTIEST STAR
RCA APBO 0001 (US).

July 1973
RETIREMENT GIG
London Hammersmith Odeon.
Intro/Hang Onto Yourself/Ziggy Stardust/Watch That Man/Wild Eyed Boy From Freecloud/All The Young Dudes/Pretty Thing/Moonage Daydream/All The Young Dudes/Pretty Thing/Moonage Daydream/Changes/ Space Oddity/My Death/Cracked Actor/ Width Of A Circle/Let's Spend The Night Together/Suffragette City/Jean Genie/ Round And Round/Rock 'n' Roll Suicide.

This is the famous retirement gig which was splashed across every music paper cover in the world.

After 'Suffragette City' Bowie announces: 'Being as this is the last show we thought we'd do something special for you . . . I know what kind of welcome you're going to give . . . Jeff Beck' then the thumping bass beat heralds Jean Genie . . . which breaks down into the old Beatles' song 'Love Me Do' for a quick two line number before returning to the mainstream Genie instrumental jam with Beck and Ronson . . . as the jam ends David took the microphone and with a sincere voice thanked the audience, the band, and the road crew saying that the tour was the greatest he'd ever done and then: 'Of all the shows on the tour this one will remain with us the longest because not only is it the last show of the tour, but it's the last show we'll ever do.' 'No,' screamed the audience as all hell broke loose in the Odeon, there were even tears as the enormity of the statement broke the hearts of the three thousand in the auditorium . . . and the band broke into a slow emotional 'Rock 'n' Roll Suicide' and the audience clapped along to the beat . . . Oh no love you're not alone . . . sing along . . . you're wonderful . . . you're not alone . . . thank you, we love you . . . and it was all over but the shouting and the tears.

September 1973
LET'S SPEND THE NIGHT TOGETHER/LADY GRINNING SOUL
RCA 0028 (US)

The retirement prompted the release of the above singles while Bowie went over to France to record his next album.

If that seems strange look again at what he said from the stage of the Hammersmith Odeon: It's the last show we'll ever do. Without treating you all like idiots the important words are *show* and *we*. On reflection what he was talking about was that it was the last show that Ziggy and The Spiders would be doing... he did NOT say that he was retiring, leaving the business never going to perform again etc. but just that things were going to change.

But of course the press couldn't have known that and what he said sounded very much as though David Bowie AKA Ziggy Stardust was hanging up his sequined jockstrap and calling it a day (quitting while he was ahead).

When he did come back it was with something very much removed from the Ziggy/Bowie we had all become used to.

September 1973
SORROW/AMSTERDAM
RCA 2424 (UK)/RCA 0160 (US)

A US demo was cut in October featuring '1984/You Didn't Hear It From Me' which was taken from the 1980 Show and is still floating around, it has the distinction of having Mick Ronson on lead guitar for the last recorded time.

October 1973
PINUPS
RCA RS 1003 (UK)/
RCA APL 1 0291 (US)
Rosalyn (Pretty Things)/Here Comes The Night (Them/Van Morrison)/I Wish You Would (Yardbirds)/See Emily Play (Pink Floyd)/Everything's Alright (The Mojos)/I Can't Explain (The Who) Friday On My Mind (The Easy Beats/ Sorrow (The Mersey Beats)/Don't Bring Me Down (The Pretty Things)/Shapes Of Things (Yardbirds)/ Anyway Anyhow Anywhere (The Who)/Where Have All The Good Times Gone (Kinks)
Producers: Ken Scott/David Bowie
Musicians: David Bowie, Mick Ronson, Trevor Bolder, Aynsley Dunbar, Mike Garson, Ken Fordenham, Juanita 'Honey' Franklin, Linda Lewis, Mac Cormack.

A complete departure from the star seeking Ziggy image which Bowie had created out of nowhere to take himself beyond the mediocre straitjacket which Decca had pushed him into in the sixties, this album is Bowie's mid-sixties re-visited.

His tribute to the music which he would have liked to have been performing on his way up.

As can be seen from the tracks and the artists (listed in brackets) Bowie has covered all that was good in the British mid sixties rock/pop; from R 'n' B with Van Morrison to The Who, with the mod mod sounds of The Pretty Things and The Kinks and the early acid-pop experiments of Pink Floyd (before they turned into cosmic starmen). It's a strange album when taken in the context of Bowie's career since 1970, but when viewed from a little further back, his formative '60s youth in the business can be seen and Pinups can be appreciated for what it is; a tribute to the past.

Reputedly there is enough material for another album (Pinups 2) in the can, recorded at the same time, but this has still to see the light of day.

October 16-18
DOLLARS IN DRAG/1980 FLOOR SHOW
1984/You Didn't Hear It From Me/Sorrow/Everything's Alright/Space Oddity/Time/Can't Explain/Jean Genie/ I Got You, Babe/Hang Onto Yourself/ Supermen/Man In The Middle.

Recorded at the Marquee Club in Wardour Street in the heart of London's Soho district, the filming took three days to complete before it was flown over to the US for broadcast the following month . . . UK audiences still have to be shown this TV special in its entirety (although short snippets have been shown on Top Of The Pops supporting a single).

This was US TV's (last?) chance to capture on film what this glitter king was doing for the benefit of their audiences . . . the fact that he had already shown those interested where he was at in long exhaustive tours around the country . . . however as far as the TV Moguls were concerned he was the big thing in 'pop' at the moment and glam-rock was worth capturing on film . . . and well, you never know, he might be taking this retirement thing seriously.

The show as it went out was breathtaking as were his many costume changes . . . one costume took the director's breath away; a legless jump suit which Bowie wore without jockstrap which, when filmed from the angle much of the show was filmed, exposed the Bowie naughty bits; Omigod! We can't show that . . . so Bowie was packed off to the dressing room to dress a little more sedately for the sensitive mid-Western ladies . . . jockstrap intact Bowie returned and the show went on.

'I Got You Babe' was a duet with occasional 'lady of pop' Marianne Faithfull, who with one hit song in the sixties surfaces regularly to produce a worthwhile album which usually goes nowhere despite the goodwill she has in the industry.

February 1974
REBEL REBEL/QUEEN BITCH
RCA LPBO 5009
Producer: David Bowie

This is the last official single featuring Mick Ronson.

The early part of the new year was a quiet period for Bowie, he went back into the studio to record his new album to be released in May.

Before the new album appeared several singles were thrown into the market to scoop up any un-committed fans lying around in preparation for the big blast on the album:

April 1974
ROCK 'N' ROLL SUICIDE/ QUICKSAND
RCA 5021 (US)
LONDON BOYS/LOVE YOU TILL TUESDAY
Decca 13579 (UK)

. . . Humm That Bowie Chappie . . . getting rather a name for himself; What! Don't we have something of his in the can? Better re-mix it into stereo . . . No no no . . . use the one from the album . . . and so the rape of the vaults began.

Although credited as Bowie & The Spiders from Mars, the A side is in fact a solo job with Bowie multi-tracking every instrument himself.

In May a little fissure was found in the Iron Curtain and a licence deal was done with the USSR on Bowie material culminating in the release of three singles:
Width Of A Circle/Cygnet Committee
Cracked Actor/John, I'm Only Dancing
All The Madmen/Soul Love

April 1974
DIAMOND DOGS
RCA APL1 0576 (UK and US)
Future Legend/Diamond Dogs/Sweet Thing/Candidate/Sweet Thing (Reprise)/ Rebel Rebel
Rock 'n' Roll With Me/We Are The Dead/1984/Big Brother/Chant Of The Ever Circling Skeletal Family
Producer: David Bowie
Musicians: Mike Garson (keyboards)
Herbie Flowers (bass guitar)
Tony Newman (drums) Earl Slick (guitar)
This album was a return to the concepts with which Bowie had so successfully built up his reputation as a rockstar prophet. Starting with a spoken introduction he introduces the theme more directly than on any previous offering.

It's a mean world sometime in the near future; the structure of Western civilisation has broken down and humanoids, split into small tribes, roam Hunger City watched from Poacher's Hill by red mutant eyes waiting for the year of the 'Diamond Dogs' – This ain't rock 'n' roll; this is Genocide.

It's straight into the title track, a driving high velocity number overwhelmed by Bowie on searing guitar every bit as good as Ronson ever used to be . . . The 'Diamond Dogs' are rockers . . . and so is Bowie . . . but in the story it's the 'year of the scavenger, the season of the bitch'.

'Sweet Thing' is almost a look back at 'The Man Who Sold The World' with Mike Garson's piano amply filling out Bowie's lament which flows into an instrumental which seems out of place and is perhaps the lowest point on the album, then 'Sweet Thing' (Reprise) returns leaving on a note of revolutionary triumph: If you want it boys Get it here free Cause hope, boys, Is a cheap thing.

A cacophony of noise precedes 'Rebel, Rebel' a love song to a tomboy teenage child of the revolution. 'Hot tramp I love you so . . . ' There's no tenderness here but exultation in her toughness.

A piano introduces the love song 'Rock and Roll With Me', which opens Side two, a love song in a decaying world with Bowie milking every drop of tragic drama out of his voice. Then it's the sadistically slow surreal number 'We Are The Dead', which owes a lot to Alice Cooper and is a song which, musically at least, could have come from Aladdin Sane, before the concept bursts into the BIG production number as electronics career madly into orchestral arrangements as Bowie's supplement to Orwell's 1984 cracks the speakers . . . it's a superb rocker.

In the end the empty humanoids see their salvation in a Big Brother for whom they will do anything just to be saved: We'll build a glass asylum, with just a bit of mayhem, Someone to claim us, someone to shame us. This fades out into an eerie chant of 'Someone to fool, someone like you, we want you Big Brother'.

The visions Bowie sees are not pretty; nothing is hunky dory in the world he sees for us, he warns us about it but offers no solutions, except that in reiterating Orwell's anti-Utopian philosophies we will be prepared to do something when the time comes.

The album was critically acclaimed, but all of the press reports were soured by criticisms of his management policy. MainMan were obstructing the press and isolating Bowie, with what were to the press, used to access to the stars, arrogant statements of the nature of 'Formal interviews are no help to journalists' and every music paper, on both sides of the Atlantic, waded into MainMan all guns blazing for what they regarded as insulting treatment.

Whether this attitude had something to do with Bowie's increasing withdrawal into himself, or to do with his appreciation of the finer things of rockstardom, namely cocaine, or whether this was a part of the MainMan powertrip and nothing to do with Bowie, will never be known. But everyone was beginning to notice that something strange was going on at MainMan . . . who seemed to be operating out of the back room at Max's Kansas City, where they allowed Bowie to meet the press with all of the clutter of New York's rock scene around him obstructing intelligent discussion.

But the word of a Bowie US tour came from Angie, at Max's Kansas City (where else) who, amongst chat of how rich old ladies would be offering her husband money to sleep with them while he was at that moment on board the SS France bound for New York . . . slipped out that the reason for coming over was to prepare for a big US tour.

May 1974
REBEL REBEL/LADY GRINNING SOUL
RCA 0287 (US)
David Bowie

MainMan took over the announcements of the forthcoming tour; Bowie would, according to press statements, be playing his longest US tour ever beginning in June, performing with a new band, The Spiders having split, he will be taking along with him a completely new concept in Rock 'n' Roll . . . ! a set designed by Jules Fisher which will transform each stage he plays on into a vision of a ruined city. The set is in pieces and designed to fit any stage, no matter how small. On it David will sing and dance his depressing vision of the future, as well as his songs of the past which catapulted him to stardom' . . . well that's what it was supposed to be:

June 1974
1984/QUEEN BITCH
RCA 10026
DIAMOND DOGS/HOLY HOLY
RCA APBO 0293 (UK and US)

The B side was cut during 'Aladdin Sane' sessions and re-hashed to make up a flip side without culling a second track from the album . . . well you never know when you might need another single to follow it up so the corporations don't queer the pitch.

The release of the title track from the album heralded the tour of the same name, which was to become Bowie's most spectacular failure yet.

Starting quietly in Montreal's Forum on June 14, and passing on to Ottawa the following day there were two days of performing the new concept-show in front of audiences before hitting Toronto and the press-corps most of whom had been flown in from around the world for 'the big comeback' since the retirement announcement in London twelve months before.

What they got was a totally new Bowie, which astounded both the press and the Ziggy-lookalike glitter public; Gone was Ziggy, here was a strange replacement, the emaciated Bowie in a double breasted Yves St Laurent suit, stylishly 'straight' haircut looking excessively respectable contrasting with the massive city-scape of a stage set which dwarfed the artist and audience.

Was 'Diamond Dogs' an extension of the Ziggy myth or not? If so what was going on? If not, why not?

What the stage-presentation was, was Bowie's dream of taking the rock concert beyond the confines of just a band on stage playing songs from an album to an audience into a theatrical extravaganza which drew the audience into the story as it unfolded on stage in grand operatic style (rock-super-opera of course!).

'Diamond Dogs' was about urban decay, and there it was, the urban landscape. It was about urban revolution and violence, and Bowie gave them it with all of the mime and special effects he could dream up. By the time he had reached 'Space Oddity' the grandest effect took Bowie up off the stage to hover above the audience clutching his mike (disguised as a red telephone!) to sing Major Tom's story, before being returned to the city for 'Diamond Dogs' itself.

Throughout the entire spectacle the band were back hidden behind the towering skyscrapers, having little or no function other than to serve as an orchestra would in an opera, to provide the music . . . gone were The Spiders from Mars and their guitarist, Mick Ronson, duelling with the 'star' for attention on stage . . . this was Bowie's party and nobody else was getting in on it.

This placing of the band was to become a major bone of contention and was a contributing factor in the collapse of the entire concept. Several excellent tapes of the tour exist;

SUBWAY
Flat Records
Rock 'n' Roll With Me/Space Oddity/Future Legend/Diamond Dogs/Panic In Detroit/Big Brother/Time/Width Of A Circle/Jean Genie

The location of the above recording is not listed on the record sleeve (the label's slogan is, incidentally, 'The Only Good record is a flat record'), but it is thought to come from that Toronto gig. The actual running order of the show was:
1984/Rebel, Rebel/Moonage Daydream/Sweet Thing/Changes/Suffragette City/Aladdin Sane/All The Young Dudes/Cracked Actor/Rock 'n' Roll With Me/Watch That Man/Drive In Saturday/Space Oddity/Diamond Dogs/Panic In Detroit/Big Brother/Time/Width Of A Circle/Jean Genie/Rock 'n' Roll Suicide.

Put that lot together and you have one powerful show. Unfortunately although it took the audiences by storm in the twenty nine cities it played, the critics while enthusiastic were . . . shall we say . . . cautiously enthusiastic about it, bringing in doubts about the concept and its method of execution along the lines of: When is a rock concert not a rock concert? and similar get out clauses to cover themselves and show that they hadn't blown their cool. They also mentioned in passing, the almost sinister presence of the 'Aladdin Sane' lightning-bolt and how it vaguely resembled a swastika.

Almost before the journalists had got over their jet-lag and were sitting down at their typewriters in London or Paris or Tokyo or wherever, the 'Diamond Dogs' Extravaganza tour was running into problems.

Two days after Toronto the show hit Detroit where there were problems with the hall's stage. Originally to be staged in the Ford Hall, the venue was changed to the smaller Cobo Hall because the stage was, of all things, too big and the illusion of the enormous city-scape backdrop would have been lost.

Tour managing an ordinary rock tour is a mass of problems; making sure everything is where it should be when it should be is no easy task, but add to that all the trappings of a Broadway big production and you've got a thousand moving parts which can all go wrong.

Journalist DJ Young didn't fly off to wherever but stayed with the tour to write about the mechanics of the operation from the inside for the (now defunct) UK magazine Let It Rock; from his report there were fifteen roadies travelling with the tour in a seedy twelve bunk-bed bus with colour TV, stereo, fridge etc. much of which didn't work . . . the only thing which did was the large quantity of cocaine which helped them through their twenty-one hour working day.

At each city the road crew were supplemented by a local union crew of twenty, and a fork lift truck. Each auditorium had a stage built by the local promoter upon which four forty-foot scaffolding towers had to be erected at either side, front and back, which would then be covered by the scenery flats of the city-scape. Then several 10 foot scaffolding platforms had to be erected out on the floor of the auditorium to house the PA. Back on stage a bridge had to be erected and a large electric motor fitted to it so that Bowie could descend from the sky. A thirty-foot steel joist which could be extended to 45ft was mounted in one of the rear towers and a chair fitted so Bowie could be lifted up over the city-scape (this had a motor and a counterweighted pivot) so that he could be extended out above the audience to the tenth row. Then the Diamond Module had to be erected; this was a mirrored, perspex contraption with wheels and an electric motor which could trundle about the stage and open like an Easter egg revealing Bowie against a mirrored interior surrounded

by fluorescent tubes. Young's daily itinerary went like this:
8am: Arrive, sort out local crew, fight over forklift. Unload 10am – 1pm: Erect stage towers, speaker towers, place speakers and lights, start wiring.
1pm: Plastic trash-can full of MacDonald's cheeseburgers and 2 trashcans beer.
1.30pm: Wire lights, speakers, amps, mixing desk. Work on special effects.
4pm: Flats erected. Lights focused. Set up band's equipment.
5pm: Four monitor systems and forty-five microphones set up. Test special effects.
6pm: Microphone test. Sound check.
7pm: Panic. Fix everything that doesn't work while munching more MacDonalds.
8pm–10pm: THE SHOW
10.30pm–12.30am: Take it all down again.
12.30am–5am: Load trucks. Search arena for roaches and discarded grass (average yield ½ ounce daily).
5.30am–8am: travel to next venue. Start again.

As can be seen from the 7pm entry, things frequently went wrong. The piece of equipment which malfunctioned most frequently was the mobile bridge which tended to jam fifteen feet above the stage leaving Bowie to hang by his fingertips and jump to the ground . . . on one occasion the brakes failed and it plummeted thirty-five feet with Bowie on it ('Is that as fast as it goes? he asked later). Now and again the Diamond Module would spin wildly round and round bumping into things. About 25% of the sound equipment had to be replaced daily due to explosions during the gigs!

The speed at which the whole thing was put together improved after the fifth day when a large shipment of cocaine arrived and the work was cut down to fourteen hours. Injury was not uncommon among the crew, although hard-hats were worn during construction . . . one crew-man fell asleep in mid-sentence at the top of one of the towers and fell to the stage fracturing his skull.

By the time the tour reached Tampa, Florida, things came apart when the driver of one of the artics 'got stung by a bee' and the special effects failed to arrive . . . Bowie took the stage, dressed casually in yellow overalls and blue sweater, and did the gig without all of the effects which he had so carefully programmed into the show . . . he even reverted to playing guitar instead of floating over the audience for 'Space Oddity', he was full of sincere apologies and the audience loved every minute of the show . . . but it was all falling apart.

By the time Philadelphia came along on July 10, the back-up band were on the point of rebellion. Sick of being hidden away behind the set, they began to wander out from behind the sheets; 'They kept bugging me about coming out in front and I kept telling them that I didn't have any parts for them and stay behind the bloody sheets!' David later explained.

The big hassle came during the Philly gigs . . . or to be more accurate about it . . . just before the Philly gigs during which the live album would be recorded, the band openly revolted and flatly refused to play when they got the news that MainMan (the management company – not The MainMan; D. Bowie) was only going to be paying them the standard union basic minimum rate of $500 . . . now that might be all right when you're using session men recruited from the want ads in the music trades . . . but when you've got Herbie Flowers, then it's a whole other ball game . . . so the band walked, and sat it out . . . dark rumblings from the MainMan office said $500 and no more, it's not as though they had to project a personality or anything . . . aha! All that 'stay behind the sheets' shit! They held out for more, MainMan dug its main heels in with managerial, suicide logic when there's a gig to do and an album to record . . . musicians learning industrial relations, negotiating tricks . . . It was only the intervention of the Mainman who got the striking band back to work again by putting his hand into the Yves St Laurent pocket and coming up with the difference between what his management were offering and what the workers wanted. But the damage had been done, the grumbling continued and the bad feeling can be heard on the record in the slightly inferior performance of the musicians . . . OK you win but stay behind the bloody sheets.

September 1974
KNOCK ON WOOD/PANIC IN DETROIT
RCA 2466 (UK)
Producer: Tony Visconti

This samba version of Panic was dropped from David Live while the B Side is the Floyd & Cropper number taken directly from the album.

It was while the above single was being released that Bowie's new stage act was being filmed for a BBC TV documentary screened in April of the following year.

October, 1974
DAVID LIVE
RCA APL2 0771 (UK)/
RCA CPL2 0771 (US)
1984/Rebel Rebel/Moonage Daydream/Sweet Thing/Changes/Suffragette City/Aladdin Sane/All The Young Dudes/Cracked Actor/When You Rock and Roll With Me/Watch That Man/Knock On Wood/Diamond Dogs/Big Brother/Width Of A Circle/Jean Genie/Rock 'N' Roll Suicide.
Producer: Tony Visconti
Musicians: David Bowie, Michael Kamen, Mike Garson, David Sanborn, Richard Grando, Herbie Flowers, Tony Newman, Pablo Rosario, Gui Andrisano, Warren Peace.

The main criticism levelled at so called 'live' albums is that they do not usually come off as anything more than poor-relations of studio records and tend to be collector-only 'greatest hits' platters, due to the technical problems of capturing the performance, mistakes and all, on tape without the acoustically perfect studio conditions – or they are so 'doctored' in a studio after the recording by re-mixing, the balances and sound levels, and even have tracks re-recorded, that they lose the spontaneity and atmosphere of the live gig and revert to being as 'artificial' as a studio album of greatest hits with irritating audience noises as a dubious bonus.

When a live album is being recorded the route the 'producer' is going to take must be clearly defined if the artist and public are going to be satisfied, even then whichever style is chosen the album will be wide open for critical attack, which is why a totally 'good' album review is seen, and why so many live albums are recorded but never see the light of day.

When the artist is using eight different mikes, and moving about the stage, the problems become worse. But Bowie and Visconti made the decision that the album was to be of the 'live' nature rather than the 'doctored' variety, and that's the way it was released . . . with one tiny exception of a thirty second break when one of the mikes failed. What came out was as close to being a truthful document of the 'Diamond Dogs' tour show (which by this time was becoming something of an albatross around Bowie's neck and was being transformed into something other than what had been planned). The differences between the bootleg Subway album and 'David Live' show was a much more Philly-sound undertone in the official album.

The tracks however do conform to the bootleg, with the exception of the addition of Eddie Floyd's 'Knock on Wood' and the deletion of 'Space Oddity', 'Drive In Saturday', 'Time' and 'Panic In Detroit' which was issued in September as a single.

The speed with which RCA put 'David Live' into the shops suggests that they were aware that the tour was being bootlegged and were determined to undercut the bootleggers with a superior product.

CRACKED ACTOR
BBC TV
Cracked Actor/Sweet Thing/Moonage Daydream/Time/Diamond Dogs/John, I'm Only Dancing/My Death/Ziggy Stardust/Rock 'n' Roll Suicide/Right

The BBC followed Bowie around with cameras and interviewer, Jeff Gold, on the abortive 'Diamond Dogs' tour. The actual concert footage comes from the LA Universal Amphitheatre, but it is so cleverly cut with shots of Bowie being driven around in ominous tinted glass limos, checking in and out of hotels, that it gives the impression that it features songs from various gigs . . . it's not a criticism, it's an inexpensive way to make a documentary. What is a criticism is the infuriating sound editing with Gold voicing over good live numbers, and the abrupt cutting to a hotel-room somewhere in LA in mid song.

Throughout the film we see another David Bowie to the one we've grown used to: he's either an introvert or an extrovert playing an introvert; in the car scene, Bowie actually seems to be shrinking away from the camera, he seems to be trying silently to escape from it by hunching up in his fur trimmed coat and pulling his fedora (a new Bowie fashion) down over his eyes.

The car appears to amplify his philosophical monologues about the existential existence of the artist as he becomes more and more remote from his public; variations on the Star-tripping theme which we've been introduced to through Ziggy and will hear more of later as he does abstract himself totally.

Out of the car, both on stage and in the hotel-room he is more relaxed as he chats about his William Burroughs style cut-up songwriting method, which he thoughtfully re-creates for the camera:

Lines, words and fragments of ideas are written down on pieces of paper, cut up and put in his fedora. Shaken and pulled out a word at a time: 'I'm an' . . . new piece . . . 'alligator' . . . and so on word for word, line by line as 'Moonage Daydream' cuts in on sound, the film is then speeded up to cleverly bring each piece of paper out of the hat as it's sung!

A bootleg tape of the film is in circulation, and it shouldn't be too long before video-bootlegs are also available. It's well worth paying for (although the BBC would probably prefer it if you didn't), since it's a fine example of what's best in the nouveau cinema-verité style of cut-up film-making pioneered in the sixties and early seventies by directors like D.A. Pennebacker, who didn't direct this!

As a footnote to 'Cracked Actor'; the TV screening was seen by film director Nicholas Roeg who thought Bowie ideal for a part in a film he was planning to make; 'The Man Who Fell To Earth', or was it 'Stranger In A Strange Land'? We'll return to that question later . . . meanwhile there were instant rumours about Bowie taking on a film role as an alien visiting Earth, which all sounds familiar.

Meanwhile the 'Diamond Dogs' abortive tour had limped its last, metamorphising as the Soul Tour which was getting underway as little by little bits of the 'Diamond Dogs' frills were dropped.

A tape of the LA gig exists independently of the BBC TV tape:

ROCK CONCERT
RCA PL 42993
Rebel, Rebel/Changes/Aladdin Sane/ All The Young Dudes/Cracked Actor/ When You Rock and Roll With Me/ Watch That Man/Diamond Dogs/ Rock 'n' Roll Suicide.
Producer: Tony Visconti

LA AMPHITHEATRE
1984/Rebel, Rebel/Moonage Daydream/ Sweet Thing/Changes/Suffragette City/ Aladdin Sane/All The Young Dudes/ Cracked Actor/Rock 'n' Roll With Me. Knock On Wood/It's Gonna Be Me/Space Oddity/Diamond Dogs/Jean Genie/Big Brother/Time/Young Americans/ John, I'm Only Dancing (Again)/ Rock 'n' Roll Suicide.

And there you have it, the artists in mid-transition, if you look closely at the second section you'll find tucked away between 'Time' and 'John, I'm Only Dancing' the give away to not only what the tour was to become, but the teaser for the next studio album; 'Young Americans' complete with sax.

The death of 'Diamond Dogs' was on the cards and seven days later a nail was driven into the coffin with the addition of black-soul back-up vocalists.

By the time the tour had wound its way back to the East Coast the city-scape and all of the props had been ditched to be replaced by a white backdrop, and the show was opened by the Mike Garson Band who warmed the audience up with hot soul before drifting almost unnoticed into 'Memory Of A Free Festival' before Bowie leapt on stage to seriously altered versions of '1984' and 'Rebel, Rebel' . . . and used the backdrop as a screen for the re-introduction of 'pure' mime shadows as he struck poses adding to the dramatic impact of the lyrics . . . the simplicity of which contrasted so starkly with the trickery and gimmickry of the earlier part of the tour.

He even introduced a whole section of the shows as being from the forthcoming album, and when the tour returned to Detroit almost four months after it left to go South and West, Bowie had taken to coming on-stage with acoustic guitar and soloing on 'Space Oddity'! Ziggy Stardust A Lad Insane was dead; re-enter Major Tom with the Disco Queen.

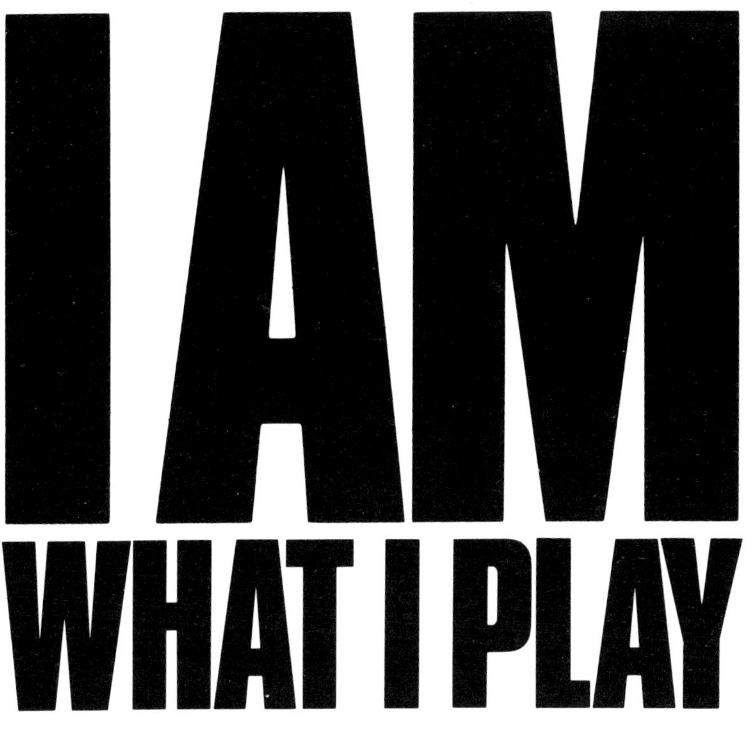

I AM WHAT I PLAY

The 1974 tour was unique on examination of all of the available material; the official albums preceding it, the live mid-tour disc, and the follow-up Young Americans, together with the bootlegs dotted all along the route, and comparing them with each other and reviews of the concerts, the gradual development of Bowie's new persona becomes exposed, the transitory stages of the metamorphosis can be traced and some understanding of what inspires the changes achieved . . . which in turn leads to a deeper comprehension of the wider aspects of what rock-music is all about. Every artist's development can be traced in a similar way, but seldom are the changes so available to the public, generally happening, as they do, behind closed doors in the privacy of the artist's home, or in the recording studio to be unveiled only when the album is released, leaving the public to speculate as to the causes of the transition, or to interviewers to probe and dig, hoping to ask the 'right' question which will spark off the 'tell-all' answer, which doesn't tell half as much as can be seen during this dramatic tour.

In some cases the transition from one musical point of view, or style is so gradual that it is only noticed by looking at the artist's first album and comparing it with the most recent, possibly ten years later, and the change is as clear as the nose on your face . . . attempts to back-track are often frustrated by gaps in the process caused by artistic or commercial decisions which delay or even obstruct the release of a vital part of the puzzle (Bob Dylan's 'Basement Tapes' lying in a CBS vault for ten years is a case in point!). The beauty of Bowie is that his about-faces and incarnations are so dramatic that they are immediately recognisable, and in the case of the '74 US 'Diamond Dogs' Soul Tour so accessible that even the casual observer cannot help but get an overview of the total picture. The BBC team had a golden chance to capture this on film but they missed it. They couldn't have known what was occurring in front of their cameras, but their film does provide moving pictures of this change . . . perhaps David Bowie's reluctance to 'open-out' for the camera was due to the fact that he didn't quite know who he was becoming . . . it didn't take him long to find out.

In a couple of hundred years when 'serious' musicologists are keying their scholarly tones into a futuristic computer or whatever . . . always assuming that

Ziggy's doom-laden predictions of decay are just scenarios of a possible future and not a veritable prophecy . . . I'd hope that they use this period to illustrate the 'rock-process', in much the same way as the folk-process is being analysed today; I have visions of a thesis being written entitled: 'The Metamorphosis of the Performing Artist in the latter Quarter of the 20th Century' and some post grad student getting a PhD out of it . . . cum laude, of course . . . but we digress.

When David Bowie came off the road at the end of '74 he had covered an amazing sixty-four concerts, starting in Montreal (July 14) and ending in Tuscaloosa, Alabama (December 2) with never more than a few days break between gigs. He must have been exhausted.

But there were slack days ahead during which he could relax and get his strength back. Popping up now and again in old 'Hollywood' style guest appearances on various radio and TV shows.

He was content to let RCA take care of putting out 'Bowie-product' and promoting it at their expense, only throwing his weight behind something if it needed him, and if he felt like it.

RCA had considerable stock in their vaults waiting for the right time; they didn't drag their feet, and early in the new year they put out the teaser:

February 1975
YOUNG AMERICANS/ SUFFRAGETTE CITY
RCA 2523 (UK)
Producer: Tony Visconti
Musicians: A side as on Young Americans LP, B side as on David Live LP.
Young Americans/Knock On Wood
RCA PB 10152 (US)
Producer and musicians as above.

The single's release was a sound commercial decision; it was the title track from the new album, which had already been cut (and was biding its time waiting for sales of David Live to tail off). Bowie had already previewed it on tour in the US and the change of style had caught the imagination of those who had heard it, and the news of a 'New Bowie' intrigued those who hadn't (i.e. most of the world). And finally it was a damn good dancing-disco single (disco is used here in the sense of a style of music . . . *not* as a dirty word). It was snapped up by the public in its tens of thousands, but although it charted in the US it still didn't reach the hot 'Number One' spot, something which had still eluded Bowie.

In March, David turned up playing his 'star' role doing a prestige guest spot on the Grammy Awards TV presentation, where although he received no award himself he had an award to present, aptly, to Aretha Franklin as best R&B singer. Aretha collected the award and obligatory kiss from the presenter, turned to the mike and said "I'm so happy I could *even* kiss David Bowie!" Oops! Foot-in-mouth, Aretha . . . it's not done to insult the guy who's just handed you a lump of metal for being good . . . well not in front of X million TV viewers who want to believe that all 'stars' are good friends really! Understandably, Bowie didn't hide his displeasure for the cameras.

Later in the evening David, playing up to the Hollywood glamour scene had his picture taken at the après-presentation party beside Art Garfunkel with Paul (Simon) and John Lennon without Paul (McCartney), but with Yoko Ono.

After the Grammy Show David receded a little, coming out only to tape an interview the following month with Radio K-ULA, before darting back in again.

This tied in nicely with the release of the new hotly over-subscribed new album:

March 1975
YOUNG AMERICANS
RCA RS 1006 (UK)
RCA APL1 0098 (US)
Young Americans/Win/Fascination/Right/ Somebody Up There Likes Me/Across The Universe/Can You Hear Me/Fame
Producers: Tony Visconti, Harry Maslin David Bowie.
Musicians: David Bowie, Dennis Davis, Andy Newmark, Emir Ksasan, Willy Weeks, Carlos Alomar, John Lennon, Earl Slick, Mike Garson, David Sanborn, Ralph McDonald, Pablo Rosario, Larry Washington, Ava Cherry, Robin Clark, Jean Fineberg, Antony Hinton, Jean Millington, Warren Peace, Dianne Sumler, Luther Vandross.

Bowie later disclaimed this album as being his 'plastic soul period', which sounded like he was putting the album down as a bad job. But in a 1978 Australian radio interview he takes his explanation further: "Hanging around 82nd Street in New York, I began to feel the emergence of a new club scene which was a disco thing." He led into overall theory of the soul-latin influences; "It wasn't just the black clubs, but it was a Puerto Rican thing too, and I got caught up in the mood of it". About the 'plastic soul' quote he laughs and continues "Yes plastic soul . . . well because it was a black-Puerto Rican thing, and I'm English I couldn't feel a part of it all, and it's a dancing scene too, I don't like to dance . . . so I just felt like I was sitting back watching it happen."

As for the title track he said: "It was really this base of music which brought 'Young Americans' out, but I sort of crammed my whole American experiences into the song and that's the way it came out" . . . in another interview he says that it's about two young newly-weds who don't quite know whether they're in love . . . well lots of people take that view of America, not being sure whether they are in love with it; both statements about the song can be taken as being valid, he crams in so many images of the USA including Nixon, and the fresh-faced youths facing the world, he even manages to draw his feelings of being an outsider into the song by fading a short portion of 'I Read the News Today', from The Beatles' Sgt Pepper's album (which John Lennon helped filter into this American experience).

'Fascination' is an out and out soul number adapted from Luther Vandross' soul hit 'Funky Music'.

'Right' is a subliminal attempt to quell the violent nature of mankind by planting an erotic mantra in its psyche . . . David's own view of the song, not the author's!

'Somebody' is a warning; or so David maintains, that there's evil about in the form of another Hitler who will use a 'god-given' right to corrupt, so beware of hero worship . . . which is, if true, ironic in the light of the shit which was to hit the fan following the release of his next studio album . . . watch the political space!

'Across the Universe' is the most surprising, and most controversial track on the album, in that it is, of course, a cover-version of The Beatles', or to be more accurate John Lennon/Beatle recorded track. It was a late addition, spur of the moment decision which began with Bowie and Lennon messing about in the studio and came out with an eminently respectable cover version which made it onto the album.

But the 'big one' of the album was a surprise to all when it was issued as a single in August:

May 1975
IMAGES
Deram DPA 3107/3108
Rubber Band/Maids of Bond Street/Sell Me A Coat/Love You Till Tuesday/There Is A Happy Land/The Laughing Gnome/The Gospel According To Tony Day/Did You Ever Have A Dream/Uncle Arthur/We Are Hungry Men/When I Live My Dream/Join The Gang/Little Bombardier/Come And Buy My Toys/Silly Boy Blue/She's Got

Medals/Please Mr Gravedigger/London Boys/Karma Man/Let Me Sleep Beside You/In The Heat of the Morning.
Producers: Mike Vernon, Tony Visconti
A low budget re-release of everything David issued during his Deram days.

August 1975
FAME/RIGHT
RCA 2597 (UK)/
RCA PB 10320 (US)
Producers: David Bowie, Harry Maslin (A side)/Tony Visconti, Harry Maslin (B side),
Musicians: see Young Americans LP.

This single is an edited down version of the actual cut which made it onto the album . . . it gave Bowie the Number One hit in the US he had been looking for. It was the result of a late-night jam with John Lennon. They decided to write a song together about management hassles . . . but obscurely . . . the basic riff started with Carlos Alomar improvising on a Bowie improvisation of 'Footstompin''. As it developed John let out little screeches "Eiie" at the relevant points; "Are you singing Fame?" cut in David. "No, I's just going "Eiie",–"Well it sounds like Fame!"– "OK," and the song just developed from that... within the framework of the fact that they were writing about management hassles... John was still immersed in the dissolution of The Beatles while David had begun to fall out with Tony Deepfreeze and MainMan.

When RCA put together their commercially successful formula of re-mixed singles and turned them into hits Bowie took himself off to the wasteland of New Mexico to film his first major starring feature film:

THE MAN WHO FELL TO EARTH
David Bowie & Candy Clark
Director: Nicholas Roeg
Written by: Walter Trevis

A sci-fi film based on Trevis' book of the same name first published in 1963 (which has more than a passing similarity in plot, theme and conclusion to Robert Heinlein's Stranger In A Strange Land, published in 1961, and was the cult book of the sixties sci-fi freaks; which goes some way to explain the confusion over which film Bowie was going to star in).

The plot centres around an alien who crash-lands in America in the present time . . . by accident . . . his scientific knowledge is so far ahead of the Earth's that he takes over American industry by coming up with so many patents so far advanced of anything already being produced (from 'instant developing film' to heavy industry) that he makes vast profits by judicial business transactions eventually becomes more powerful than Howard Hughes and The President put together.

As the story develops we are shown flashbacks to his home planet; an arid New-Mexico like landscape with his family dying through lack of water and the viewer can only suspect that Thomas Jerome Newton (the alien aka Bowie) is on a mission of mercy, but the crash screwed up his plans. He uses his wealth and power to get a space programme off the ground (so to speak) which we can only suspect is aimed at getting him back to his nuclear family up there somewhere . . . I say suspect, because this film is so confused, that nothing is ever made clear . . . it's further complicated by a total of twenty-three minutes cut from the original print . . . which may have made it a little clearer . . . but having also read the book I doubt it!

Anyway, somewhere along the road to the stars Newton picks-up a 'dumb broad' in the shape of Candy Clark giving a lot of footage of tempestuous arguments and torrid (but not explicit) sex, during which Bowie bares all flashing his pubic hair . . . back to the plot (plot!?) His lady discovers that he has a family 'back home' and blows the gaff on his plans to abandon the earth . . . he is thwarted at the last moment and put through an indoctrination programme (which seems liberally borrowed from Clockwork Orange . . . down to the chair and flashing images) . . . Newton's resistance caves in and, realising that his family have probably croaked by now, gives up and decides to stay on Earth where the grass is greener . . . the final shot suggests that he is making a bid for the 'pop' world as he meets his ex-business advisor in a roof-top restaurant with a copy of his new album, which is alluded to in passing.

The whole film is alluded to in passing, or should be forgotten in passing except for the fact that it does star David Bowie in the lead role. It is therefore of interest.

Bowie's acting is of the mahogany variety, a little wooden, delivering his lines with the precision and concentration of an actor not totally at ease with the camera, and, by no stretch of the imagination, could he be compared with Sir Lawrence Olivier or Richard Burton.

In the movie industry, The Man Who Fell To Earth is regarded with amusement and thought of as having novelty value because it does feature that 'pop star' David Bowie, and in the music press it was regarded as a total failure, not because of Bowie's part, but because of the total lack of cohesiveness, and meanderings of a thinly spread script.

From a personal point of view, I understood it despite the book, and viewing it twice, but because I had read Heinlein's Stranger In A Strange Land . . . and work that out for yourself; I had to!

September 1975
SPACE ODDITY/CHANGES/ VELVET GOLDMINE
RCA 2593 (UK)

This re-release in RCA's Maximillion series took off in a big way and gave David his first ever British number one in November. With 'Fame' having topped the US charts two months previously, David had reached a commercial peak that was both elating and disturbing at the same time.

Back in the 'real' world of Rock 'n' Roll David went back into the Studios to lay down another album, this time keeping the identity of the 'featured mask' a secret for as long as possible, well for about two months until RCA released:

November 1975
GOLDEN YEARS/CAN YOU HEAR ME
RCA 2640 (UK)/RCA PB 10441 (US)

Producers: David Bowie, Harry Maslin

There was no real secret to keep, Golden Years is a direct progression from the Young Americans Philly-sound. The single version is an edited down copy of the strongest track on the forthcoming album . . . the plan had worked well with Heroes, didn't it?

The flip side is culled from Young Americans, and gives nothing away about the new album.

A strange feeling of anticipation was gripping Bowie-fans as they awaited the issue of each new album, not just the usual feelings of fans waiting to hear new songs, but that of fans waiting to determine just who Bowie was going to be this time around . . . what they got on record wasn't all that different from the previous album . . . but the side effects of who Bowie was interpreted as becoming stunned and stung both critics and public alike, he was emerging as the anti-hero in one of his own scenarios . . . but off-stage . . . and a dark cloud still hangs over this album as a result.

STATIONTOSTATIONDAVIDBOWIE

January 1976
STATION TO STATION
RCA APL1-1327 (UK and US)
Station to Station/Golden Years/Word On A Wing/TVC 15/Stay/Wild Is The Wind
Producers: David Bowie, Harry Maslin
Musicians: David Bowie, Carlos Alomar, Earl Slick, Roy Bitt, George Murray, Dennis Davis.

Originally entitled The Return of the Thin White Duke, Bowie recorded this at the Cherokee Studios in Hollywood where it is a mixture of US and European influences; which is exactly what Bowie was looking for. The Thin White Duke is a shadowy figure which we all have inside of us, figures Bowie; what he intended was that it would be about an English expatriate returning home to rediscover his roots.

Unfortunately for David his return, which was intended as a triumphal re-entry and started off that way, with one paper headlining their story 'David the Goliath/The Messiah', turned sour when the press saw him; David Bowie dressed in brown shirt, narrow tie with a small knot, and what appeared to be jackboots. One paper put that together with a photo of David's arrival at a London station where he looks very much as though he is giving a Nazi salute . . . and they made five.

While he had been in the US and touring the world, the UK and London in particular had been infested by a vicious political doctrine which, under the guise of a 'new' political party; the National Front, had been recruiting on the basis of racial hatred particularly amongst the very kids who followed Ziggy's god-like rise. The Front did not even attempt to hide their blackshirt attitudes but flaunted them with fascist salutes behind Union Jacks and 'Britain for the British' slogans; later the same year it led to full-scale riots in the streets with the Anti-Nazi League and National Front (National Socialist?). Police brought out riot shields for the first time in British mainland peace-time. It was and is a growing hateful movement.

So when David Bowie came back looking like the typical Aryan, flashing what could have been construed as fascist salutes, is it any wonder that it seemed like an invasion of Poland was imminent? The kids in the Front were looking for a rock star to give them the word... Clapton and Ray Davis had already been suckered into making right-wing, almost extremist statements, and now Ziggy, the Clockwork-Orange Superman had come out and made a stand.

Fortunately, Bowie put these suggestions that he had Nazi leanings down when they arose, and has continued to do so when asked: 'I hate Nazism and all it stands for, he said in one interview, and even went as far as to name the National Front as a Nazi organisation which he wanted no part of... which is as well for him, his popularity would have dwindled and even if it hadn't this is one book which would never have been written!

Even if his 'salute', which he claims was an accident... he was caught in mid-wave... was a joke; it damaged his image and it raised a doubt about what he's been singing about all these years; you don't Fuck with Fascism... sorry to be so heavy but it is important, crucially so. But to return to the album:

'Golden Years' is a return to the latin/soul influences of Young Americans, a quick shuffling samba-rhythmed song about the artist's paranoia of failure while

at the top ... a sure-fire disco single.

'TVC 15' is a strange complicated song which is best explained by Bowie himself: 'It's about a hologramic TV, "my" girlfriend jumps into it and becomes absorbed by it, and rather than live without her "I" crawl into it to be with her.' ... simple isn't it?

Bowie described 'Word On A Wing' as his acceptance of the inevitable and 'Stay' follows the (recurring) theme of the artist's isolation and paranoia of 'Golden Years'. The final track on the album was not written by Bowie but by Ted Washington and Dimitri Tiomkin.

Between the recording of 'Station To Station' and its release Bowie slipped in two TV appearances which turned out to be mildly controversial, each for their own reasons:

November 28 **The Russell Harty Show**
BBC TV

Nothing too musically controversial came out of this rather limp satellite interview across the Atlantic. Standard chat show questions got standard chat show answers.

But where the show did raise a stir was in the very nature of the broadcast ... Generalissimo Franco, Dictator of Spain, since 1938, the last of the 'big three' fascists, after weeks of being plugged in to all of the life-support systems medicine could find to attach to him, died that day, and when asked to give up his satellite time so that America could receive the pictures of the jubilant/mourning crowds in the Madrid Streets, Bowie refused.

Whether it was out of a political stance, or just a selfish media-hogging rock-star's ego, we can't be sure, but in the light of all the shit which was to come down on his head in the ensuing six months, I'd like to believe it was the former. The second TV gig was on the black-oriented music programme aired in the US:

December **Soul Train TV Show**

Bowie had earlier laughed off suggestions that his musical direction would lead him into the Soul Train studios. But just after recording 'Station To Station' there, he was in an all black studio lip synching to 'Golden Years' and 'Fame' (the singles' versions of course).

He also did a short interview where he explained his roots in R&B back in Brixton where he hung out on street corners, popped pills (blues probably) and listened to James Brown ... when he was seventeen ... so this new soul-Bowie was not a new Bowie but an old Bowie.

Then suddenly, almost a year after his last live performance, the new Bowie road-show hit Toronto again at the start of yet another long haul around the US, starting on February 2, crossing over to the West Coast to slide down from Seattle to San Diego (taking in points along the way), before hooking back across the South East back up to Canada, wandering around the Midwest and the South for a while finally coming to rest in New York on March 26 having played thirty-three concerts in the sixty-odd days!

This was the Thin White Duke Tour, which differed slightly in image from the tail end of the Soul Tour. A good example of the performances given are featured on:

WISH UPON A STAR
Bowie '76
Wizardo
Waiting For The Man/Word On A Wing/Stay/TVC 15/Panic In Detroit/Changes/Fame/Diamond Dogs.

This very good quality album comes from the February 9, LA Forum gig and is about as good a representation of the gigs as you'll get, even considering that there is one track, 'Sister Midnight', missing.

If coupled with another Wizardo album gives across the board coverage of most of Bowie's touring stock numbers:

THE THIN WHITE DUKE
Wizardo
IMP114
Station To Station/Suffragette City/Fame/Word On A Wing/Stay/Panic In Detroit/Changes/TVC 15/Diamond Dogs/Rebel, Rebel/Jean Genie/Can You Hear Me/Young Americans
Recorded from the live radio stereo broadcast on K-BFH of the Nassau, NY, March 24 gig, it covers most tracks (regrettably leaving out 'Sister Midnight' again). But does include as the last two tracks the numbers from the November 23, 1975 Cher Show.

It will be seen from the songs played that Bowie was reaching back into his past to put together his playlist for the shows rather than concentrate upon the previous two albums... this was a wise decision since much of his audiences were made up of young teeny-bopper converts who turned onto Bowie with the hit single 'Fame' and by introducing them to the older stuff pointed them towards the solid back-list.

At the end of the US tour Bowie came over to Europe to work with Brian Eno on an album in Berlin, and it was at the start of May when the Nazi shit hit the fans.

Bowie managed to put the tour together in Europe, starting with four gigs in Germany, on to Switzerland, Sweden and ending with three concerts at the Empire Pool, Wembley, London on May 3, 5 & 7.

The last of these was captured on tape and appears on a Japanese bootleg:

DON'T TOUCH THAT DIAL
Marc
Station To Station/Suffragette City/Fame/Word On A Wing/Stay/Waiting For The Man/Queen Bitch/Life On Mars/Changes/TVC 15/Diamond Dogs

For sheer emotional power this is the bootleg of the tour, the last gig and the first time he had been back in London on-stage since the 1973 Retirement gig. The producers of official 'live' albums could learn a thing or two about presenting live gigs on album, this achieves the balance between good sound reproduction and overwhelming atmosphere.

After the end of the tour David went to Berlin to see what Brian Eno was doing... it's at this point that Bowie's characterisations start taking over again... if he had been called a Nazi for the way he dressed, he was again changing, going back in time to the early thirties' decadent Germany for inspiration (which would emerge a few years later on celluloid with his next feature film).

What came out of Berlin and the collaboration with Eno, which would continue for more than just one album, perplexed many of his new fans who loved him for 'Fame', and many of his older die-hard followers who were used to his changes. It was the result of a growing dissatisfaction with his lot in life, or in the music scene at least. Bowie had become RCA's safe bet, a guarantee of minimum sales. He took no real chances; his characterisations didn't really present a challenge to him or his public in musical terms; Space-rock, Soul, Disco were all operating within well trodden, acceptable paths, all Bowie did was do what any artist working within the framework of a musical classification does, he made the best of the framework, altered the internal structure without actually altering the structure itself.

The tour – album – tour – album syndrome of the previous few years were honing down the rough edges and making him less and less open to experimentation. Those who were experimenting were not commercially 'big' in sales terms, but they were satisfied in themselves that they were challenging the boundaries of music, breaking the rules and expressing themselves. Unfortunately the great mass of the public didn't feel that the music produced expressed their personal experiences, and so left them to get on with it and only the intellectuals attempted to follow them.

April 1976
TVC 15/WE ARE THE DEAD
RCA 2682 (UK)/RCA PB 10664 (US)
Producers: David Bowie, Harry Maslin (A side)/David Bowie (B side)

'TVC 15' grazed the Top Forty in the UK making it to No 33 before plummetting straight out again while 'Stay' didn't even get that far.

Bowie had spent a year and a half in LA and had become immersed in 'the scene'. 'I surrounded myself with people who indulged my ego,' he said of the period later. 'They treated me as though I was Ziggy Stardust or one of my characters, never realising that David Jones might be behind it. I had a more-than-passing relationship with drugs... actually I was zonked out of my mind. You can do good things with drugs, but then comes the long decline. I was skeletal. I was destroying my body.'

Living in Bel Air he was playing with giant inflatable sculptures, one of which was fifteen feet tall and had its foot stuck through a globe, and a penis of 3-D postcards of LA with a Mickey Mouse sharpener at the end.

'I was endowed with a good friend,' he said, 'who stood me in front of a mirror and he said 'I'm walking out of your life because you're not worth the effort'... after that humiliation I went to my wardrobe closet and locked all my characters inside.'

He left LA and took himself off to England which was in many respects a mistake because of the criticism he came under there. He was seeking a friend or a set of people who would treat him as a human and not a star machine ... he was also looking for artistic expressionism from a self pleasing intellectual point of view.

One of the avant-gardists on the music scene was Brian Eno who had been one of the founder members of

Roxy Music, but left the band due to a falling out with Brian Ferry about the function of his electronics in the band. He then took his synthesizer off and joined the avant-garde. Bowie being on the fringe (but still within the sphere of rock) was open to a challenge and so the two started to get something together in Berlin.

Bowie said of Berlin: 'I wanted to go somewhere I felt an alien. Where I didn't know the people, and where I felt in conflict... I write better like that, in a city with which I'm not familiar... New York and LA had become too familiar; not too dull, but I knew them too well to write.'

Of the collaboration Eno said that they rarely saw each other in the studio since they tended to work at different times.

Out and about in Berlin with his prodigy, Iggy Pop, he soon soaked up the flavour of the Berlin-underground low life; the Nightclubs, the Cabarets, the Strip/Fuck shows with the neo-expressionism which still hung in the city air even after the war and partition into East and West. It was a frontier city, not just politically but culturally and artistically. Bowie had returned to his 'artistic' decadent environment... a little like the club scenes in Cabaret. There was nothing warm and comfortable about Berlin art, it had the austerity of Brucke and the definition of Man Ray... it was and is 'ice art', a sort of last grasp at life, with the angst of the German art-world Bowie could kick his cocaine habit and wallow in the arts-lab movement again... indeed he returned to painting with acrylics. And allow his hair to turn back to its original light brown.

While in Europe, RCA pitched in with a 'best of' type album which was notable only for being a corporate album, one that has been put together with one eye on the till, because it was devoid of any hint of Bowie in the organisation or arrangement of tracks:

May 1976
CHANGESONEBOWIE
RCA RS 1055 (UK)/
RCA APL 1 1732 (US)
Space Oddity/John I'm Only Dancing/Changes/Ziggy Stardust/Suffragette City/The Jean Genie/Diamond Dogs/Rebel Rebel/Young Americans/Fame/Golden Years
Producer & Musicians: Various

This is David Bowie squared off and stripped of the concepts around which the songs were based and put together again for the new fans who didn't want to wade through the costly back-list.

'Fame' and 'Golden Years' have brought Bowie within the reach of a huge teen market and RCA weren't going to let them get away too easily: So you put together an almost random collection of tracks from previous albums and wait for them to like each song and go looking for the album it comes from... makes sense doesn't it?

Unfortunately, it's strictly for the kids; the inclusion of the previously unreleased (in the US) 'John, I'm Only Dancing' was the only attraction to the bulk of Bowie's older followers, who had built up a resentment towards his younger 'fans' although they themselves had been these fans before 'Fame' hit the heights!

It's not really worth talking about any further.

July 1976
SUFFRAGETTE CITY/STAY
RCA 2726 (UK)

August 1976
STAY/WORD ON A WING
RCA PB 10736 (US)

In Britain RCA re-released 'Suffragette City' to help promote Changesonebowie, while in America 'Stay' was an attempt to capitalise further on the success of 'Fame'.

January 1977
LOW
RCA PL 12030 (UK)/
RCA APL 12030 (US)
Speed Of Life/Breaking Glass/What In The World/Sound And Vision/Always Crashing In The Same Car/Be My Wife/A New Career In A New Town Warszawa/Art Decade/Weeping Wall/

Subterraneans
Producers: Tony Visconti/David Bowie
Musicians: David Bowie, Carlos Alomar, Dennis Davis, George Murray, Eno, Robert Fripp, Roy Young, Ricky Gardener, Eduard Meyer.

This is a difficult album to come to grips with, unless you are into the machine music of bands like Kraftwerk or Tangerine Dream or Frip and Eno.

Side Two is the hardest to comprehend since the first track is an instrumental conceptual piece based upon Bowie and Eno's visit behind the Iron Curtain to Warsaw (to state the obvious 'Warszawa' is Warsaw in Polish!). Any attempt to analyse it makes one sound like an earnest young German intellectual complete with thin pencil beard going on at length about art-and-the state... it's a grim depressing little number which is followed by another grim depressing number 'Art Decade' (Art Deco – Art Decade... getit?), like its name-derivative it is crisply mechanical; there are no soft lines or forms as in Art Nouveau; it is functional art to a fault, and applied as music it is too functional to be taken seriously (except by the earnest German lurking around the critic's room). 'Weeping Wall'; an obvious title for a track recorded in Berlin... the wall isn't the livingroom wall that's for sure. 'Subterraneans; same sort of thing.

Side One is more like the Bowie we're used to, but he's showing signs of another change, which he later claimed was the start of 'himself' breaking out, and indeed he said that he never attempted to create another person on an album again. 'Speed Of Life' throws away the paranoia of previous days and replaces it with super confidence, just as manic though! 'Breaking Glass' is a song which hints at the collapse and tantrums of a relationship, perhaps his management deal with Walter Lipman... it contains the line: You're such a wonderful person, but you've got problems... which is quite a put-down; You're a wunnerful poison! 'What In The World' has Iggy doing backup vocals and is basically a look at the Sixties generation which spawned 'Diamond Dogs' and the revolution it looked towards, and asks: 'OK you blew it... what now?'

'Sound And Vision' is the only really marketable track on the whole thing; a cut up song of extreme proportions. 'Always Crashing In The Same Car' is unmistakably about suicide, not of the Rock 'n' Roll variety; glorious and majestic, but dull and repetitive – artistic, what he must have felt about all of that touring in the US. 'Be My Wife' is exactly that, while the last track is another instrumental whose title suggests that he regarded what he was doing as something more worthwhile than anything before and worth continuing, 'A New Career In A New Town'.

In all it's not an album I'd want for a friend; one critic said that it was music to have a bath to, not as the subtitle suggests 'New Music: For The Night And Day'.

RCA were less than pleased when he presented them with it, here they buy the new material, there is more resilience with the Bowie public than he gave them credit for, they went into their record shops and, ignored, actually bought the single. It got good radio airplay and edged into the charts (much to Bowie's chagrin, I assume).

Bowie's statements about not wanting the public to buy the single or the album, were not, as some critics have suggested a mere ploy to draw the punters in to find out what in the world he didn't want them to hear, but were typical of the 'serious' artist nature of Bowie's feelings at the time; the artists of the particular Subterranean movement which he had joined, considered 'art' to be for the few who had the intellectual capacity to appreciate it... generally only themselves and their group of friends... most certainly not for mass consumption but 'art' by a clique for a clique... anti-social-art... being a part of that Bowie's statements ring true.

March 1977
Iggy Pop
THE IDIOT
RCA APL 1-2275
Sister Midnight/Nightclubbing/Fun Time/China Girl/Dum Dum Boys/ Tiny Girl/Baby/Mass Production

This album, although not a 'Bowie' album *per se* does merit inclusion in the scheme of things since David did write most of the music, and performs throughout playing sax and guitar.

It was the result of a collaboration between Iggy and Ziggy which goes back a long way. Iggy the first 'punk' (in the British anarchic vein) took on an almost alter-ego role for Bowie who wanted Iggy to succeed despite his strange stage grovellings and outrageous drug stupors.

So much did Bowie want Iggy to make it that when he next took the stage on tour it was as a backing musician for Iggy: Again starting way up in Canada Bowie took Iggy through a sixteen gig trek through North America, on which he refused to be drawn into the limelight ... it was Iggy's tour.
Even a spot on the Dinah Shore Show couldn't induce the Star out of his role of sideman. Bootlegs of this tour appear as:

IGGY & ZIGGY (Seattle April 9)
DB Pop Stereo Label
Medley 1969/No Fun/96 Tears/Gimme Danger/Calling Sister Midnight/Search & Destroy/I Wanna Be Your Dog/ China Girl.

SUCK ON THIS
Iggy & Ziggy
Raw Power/TV Eye/Dirt/1969/Turn Blue/Fun Time/Gimme Danger/No Fun/ Sister Midnight/I Need Somebody/ Search & Destroy/I Wanna Be Your Dog/ Lust For Life/The Passenger/ Nightclubbing/1, 2 Brown Eyes.

By August, sales of 'Sound And Vision' were tailing off and the new product had to be released if all was not to be lost with the plummetting sales of Low:

June 1977
BE MY WIFE/SPEED OF LIFE
RCA PB 1017 (UK)/RCA PB 11017 (US)

Another minor 'hit' which scratched the surface of the lower end of the UK charts; but he turned up for a UK Top Of The Pops, his first venture out into the world again as David Bowie, and not just sideman for Iggy.

His TV appearance was amazing, in that he still managed to command his old stage presence in such a plastic environment. Top Of The Pops is pre-recorded in a sound studio where the musicians can get their numbers exactly right, and then the acts lip-synch to the backing track and go through their movements for the camera ... this is a well established format for the programme ... a variation on the old acting theory that many actors can't walk and chew gum at the same time ... the union won't allow them to use their records to lip-synch to. Anyway he put the mediocre batch of aspiring teen idols to shame by getting it so right first time!

September 1977
HEROES/V2 SCHNEIDER
RCA PB 1121 (UK)/RCA PB 11121 (US)
This edited version of 'Heroes' was re-recorded in French and German for those markets.

Ostensibly telling us all that we could all be heroes, the song comes from a scene Bowie saw while in Berlin; 'I saw two kids, about nineteen or twenty meeting at the Wall under a gun turret every day', he said in an interview with Rolling Stone's Charles M Young. 'They were obviously having an affair of some kind. There were much better places to meet so why did they choose a gun turret? I assumed their motive was guilt, thus

the act of heroism in facing it'...
'of course it could just be my wonderful imagination. Probably their offices were nearby!'

Despite its message and the fact that it was a damn good song it only made it to No 24 in the UK charts hanging around for eight weeks.

October 1977
HEROES
RCA PL 12522 (UK)/
RCA AFL 12522 (US)
Beauty And The Beast/Joe The Lion/ Heroes/Sons Of The Silent Age/ Blackout.
V-2 Schneider/Sense Of Doubt/Moss Garden/Neukoln/The Secret Life Of Arabia.
Producers: David Bowie, Tony Visconti
Musicians: David Bowie, Carlos Alomar, Dennis Davis, George Murray, Eno, Robert Fripp.

To my mind this album is less difficult to come to grips with than 'Low'... but it still isn't that easy. The first track 'Beauty And The Beast' is about the compulsion of beauty and ugliness found in the children's story 'You can't say no more to the beauty and the beast'. 'Joe The Lion' is a little more involved (if the liner notes on Bowie Now promo disc are to be believed it 'illustrates the future panic and social disintegration'... well then!).

'Sons Of The Silent Age' is a tune to the disaffected youth who were coming out of the London backstreets and landing record contracts in the '76-'77 Punk boom in the UK... as they embraced anarchy Bowie was looking around for a cause to give them to replace it (rather high handed of him), but he does revive his Cockney accent as a step towards them. The first side ends with 'Blackout' which is not about Bowie's blackout (which could be expected) but quite simply a song about the New York blackout and the panic it caused amongst the regular Joe in the street... of course Bowie looked at this from Berlin and saw what he wanted to see... rape, mugging, death, fear and a population explosion... a city gone mad.

The second side starts with the cryptically entitled 'V-2 Schneider', the V-2 was a missile thrown at London in the latter days of the Second World War and Schneider is the Florian Schneider of Kraftwerk whom Bowie was musically flirting with... put together and 'V-2 Schneider' seems to say it all.

A personal note: I tend to think that the metal machine musik has no real humanity and robs its musicians of their willingness to communicate with their public. It is curious that while Bowie, who has always attempted to give his fans a message and a vision of the future, was playing around with soulless robot musik, the kids at street level in his home town were screaming into mikes in recording studios all over London that not only had anarchy arrived and was taking over but Bowie's vision of the 'Diamond Dogs' was actually being enacted in the streets with packs of society's rejects provoking the establishment into confusing attitudes to their rebellion; not quite sure of how to absorb it into their structuralised busines they were simultaneously paying through the nose to get a piece of the action and banning it refusing to honour contracts holding back release of records and coming down with the full weight of big business and the law to try to somehow rub off the rough edges; calling it New Wave instead of Punk was a start... and what was Bowie doing? Playing sincere artistic robot philosopher in Berlin... each to his own. The rest of the album follows Bowie's eclectic introspection.

November 1977
BING CROSBY CHRISTMAS SHOW
Little Drummer Boy – Peace On Earth/Heroes

Bowie and Bing recorded the 'Little Drummer Boy – Peace On Earth' medley for Christmas 1977 but Bing died before Christmas came around, so the special was screened in the US in November (in the UK it was put out at the allocated time).

Bowie put in a somewhat stilted performance keeping to the rehearsed script, but when it came to singing he proved that he had everything the Old Crooner had, the high notes on the

'Peace On Earth' section are amazing. This is one bootleg which should find its way onto an official compilation album sometime, if there is any justice in the world.

January 1978
BEAUTY AND THE BEAST/ SENSE OF DOUBT
RCA PB 1190 (UK)/RCA PB 11190 (US)
Producers: David Bowie, Tony Visconti

The rumours were flying again about Bowie's future projects, he would or would not be touring the US, would or wouldn't be recording with Devo, would or wouldn't be divorcing Angie, would or wouldn't be filming again ... this time a movie entitled Wally about German expressionist painter Egon Schiele.

What he did come up with was beyond the imagination of any of his fans:

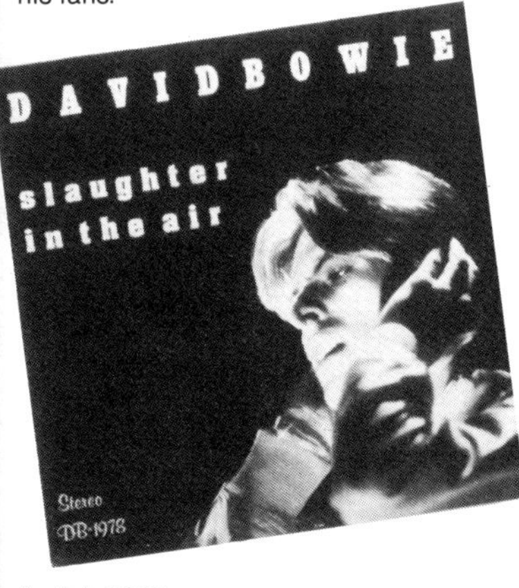

April 4, 1978
SLAUGHTER IN THE AIR
Los Angeles Forum
Heroes/What In The World/Be My Wife/ Jean Genie/Blackout/Sense Of Doubt/ Speed Of Life/Breaking Glass/Beauty And The Beast/Fame/Five Years/ Soul Love/Star/Hang Onto Yourself/ Ziggy Stardust/Suffragette City/Rock 'n' Roll Suicide/Art Decade/Stay/TVC-15/ Rebel, Rebel (includes 'Helden & Heroes', French version).

Starting slow and easy with 'Warszawa', Bowie forced them to quieten down and give his new music a chance, before coming on to do the one real hit of recent times, 'Heroes', dressed in polyester pants and fluorescent green t-shirt he looked like the result of a headlong clash between Yves St Laurent and PUNK ... he never looked anything less than chic with his perpetual Gitanne high camp.

Weaving in and out of his older material the new stuff is laid on the audience, not as a comparison, but more of a demonstration that the early songs were out of the ordinary in their day (although not quite this much out of the ordinary!). It also gave those who had come over to Bowie from the Kraftwerk camp, a look at what he had been doing before his Berlin period.

Lit with the back-drop of the niew-musik, the glaring neon strip-light, he demonstrated their effectiveness with the older rock as he suddenly brought Ziggy onstage for a guest appearance before putting him back in the box in favour of a little more angst ridden art ... and then ending on an upper with 'Rebel, Rebel'.

The tour continued after the May Madison Square gigs in New York. He brought the whole thing over to Europe, starting in Frankfurt and passing through France, Scandinavia and Scotland before arriving at London's Earls Court.

May 1978
David Bowie Narrates Prokofiev's 'Peter and the Wolf' with Eugene Ormandy and The Philadelphia Orchestra.
RCA Red Seal LR 12743

RCA were looking around for a narrator for Prokoviev's introduction to the orchestra in fairy tale style, and David jumped at the chance to do it as a present for his son, Zowie.

He narrated the script in almost one take back in LA, adding nothing ... well perhaps the bit about the hunters shooting the wolf with shotguns ... the script said rifles but Bowie believed that the kids would go for shotguns, and shotguns it became.

During the breaks between recording he had been giving an interview to Rolling Stone, extolling the virtues of Berlin and how whatever he does in the future is going to be misunderstood.

'I get bored after the first twelve gigs,' he said. 'I have no characters to do this time... I have a commitment to the old songs but I don't know how I'll do them without the characters... I have no wish to tart them up, it will be just me and the music'... as for the misunderstandings: 'I don't care, I have less formulated ideas about my life than ever'. When asked why, if he was enjoying life so much and doing what he pleased, was he returning to the circus, he answered: 'Very simple – I need the money.'

Again starting early in the year Bowie geared up to take his new musical style on the road, confident that with two albums supporting it it was now ready for live audiences.

Starting in Southern California he took the long way around the US playing twenty-five cities in the three months March April and May.

Spring 1978
BOWIENOW
RCA Promo-disc
V-2 Schneider/Always Crashing In The Same Car/Sons Of The Silent Age/ Breaking Glass/Neukoln/Speed Of Life/ Joe The Lion/What In The World/ Blackout/Weeping Wall/Secret Life Of Arabia.

With the sales of 'Low' and 'Heroes' disappointing RCA had to pull some rabbits out of the hat fairly sharply to pull commercial success out of a rout. So the promo-disc was swung into the battle.

The promo-disc is nothing new, in fact it's a well worn ploy to get as much radio airplay out of a product which isn't getting what the company think is enough (payola is the other method). Basically the promo-disc is cut for limited release to DJs, thus creating a desirable and collectable product... fuelling the egos of DJs that they should be on the promo-disc mailing list (and are therefore important people)... draws attention to an artist who isn't doing too much or is touring without a product. In this case the disc is a compilation of the two previous albums, makes it easier to play a track from each album in the one show without having to cue up two separate decks.

It had limited success and sales stayed below par.

While his albums were flopping in the record shops of the world Bowie was pursuing his other career – acting.

JUST A GIGOLO
Leguan Films (Berlin)
David Bowie, Sydne Rome, Maria Schell, Kim Novak, Marlene Dietrich.
Director: David Hemmings

Paul, the newly recruited and inducted junior lieutenant arrives at the front line trenches shortly before the 1918 armistice is called, just in time it appears to see one short piece of action; getting blown up (but not very damaged). He returns home to Berlin, not quite the conquering hero, not even a defeated hero, in fact he arrives a little confused with his only possession, a live pig, which he carries in his arms like a struggling baby.

His only asset in this depressed defeated Germany was that he is a Prussian, an officer, and above all pretty. He quickly gets seduced by Kim Novak and drawn into the Gigolo circuit where he is 'managed' by Marlene Dietrich. Paul gets immersed in decadent Berlin until he is killed by a stray bullet in one of those fracas they were having in the late 1920s in Berlin between the Communists and Nazis.

Interestingly, although Bowie co-stars with Dietrich, he doesn't actually co-star with her. She had her scenes shot in Paris and his shots were made in Berlin. They were then brought together by the wonders of the modern film cutting room... Kim Novak and Bowie did meet however as will be obvious from the seduction scene.

Bowie later said that he enjoyed the film more than the shooting of The Man Who Fell To Earth: It is more comprehensible, being as the story line can be followed without any of the obvious obscurities of the former.

In playing the part Bowie seemed to have found another 'look' for himself, his lank gaunt features did look the part when placed in a dinner jacket, white dickie tie and white silk scarf; with hair slicked back it was certainly more fitting than the fifties' gangster-look he had for a while. His appearance disturbed Kim Novak (remember he *did* meet her) and tried to fatten him up 'Everybody wants to look after my health; David is reputed to have said about it... sounds like it came right out of the press-office up there at Warner-Columbia if you ask me. The pig kept shitting on him too! The film was a commercial flop.

Back in the world of rock music, the Boys at RCA were getting more than a little worried, sales were bad, recession was looming, this punk thing was getting out of hand... America wanted it but it wasn't a new craze put together by the

record companies in conjunction with the hula-hoop company, it was a street level rebellion. Either you were born into the street and been unemployed socially deprived or you weren't... and those who weren't buying from the multi-nationals but from small self-help instant labels formed by the bands and their mates outside the Soho Square Mile of record companies. It was a worrying time for the major companies.

Bowie wasn't helping, his sales weren't up to their usual standard and he wasn't touring and he was going around telling people he didn't want them to buy the records which weren't selling... what kind of way was that to go about it? Time to have a chat with the boy.

September 1978
STAGE
RCA PL 02913 (2) (UK)
RCA CPL 22913 (US)
Hang On To Yourself/Ziggy Stardust/ Five Years/Soul Love/Star
Station To Station/Fame/TVC 15/ Warszawa/Speed Of Life/Art Decade/ Sense Of Doubt/Breaking Glass/ Heroes/What In The World/Blackout/ Beauty And The Beast
Producers: Tony Visconti, David Bowie
Musicians: David Bowie, Carlos Alomar, Dennis Davis, George Murray, Adrian Belew, Simon House, Sean Mayes, Roger Powell.

The hassles around Bowie and saleable product held up the release of the live album from the Spring '78 tour until October. It would appear that Bowie wanted the album to count as two records towards his contracted number, since it's a double. This sort of haggling generally goes on when an artist is coming towards the end of his contract and wants to re-negotiate or move to another company, so it looked as though there were storm clouds gathering behind the scenes.

September, 1978
LIZA JANE/LOUIE LOUIE GO HOME
Decca F13807 (UK)
Producer: Les Conn
Panning for gold in their vaults, Decca made a half hearted attempt at promoting this re-release of David's début single and it got nowhere.

November 1978
BREAKING GLASS/ART DECADE, ZIGGY STARDUST
RCA BOW 1(UK)
Producers: David Bowie, Tony Visconti
RCA honoured David with a personalised catalogue number for this and future releases. It was taken from the 'Stage' album.

By the time 'Stage' appeared, Bowie had taken the tour over to Japan and Australia where several good quality bootlegs were taped:

November 18, 1978
KISS YOU IN THE RAIN
Melbourne, Australia
Jean Genie/Be My Wife/Five Years/ Soul Love/Star/Hang Onto Yourself/ Fame/Beauty And The Beast/Alabama Song/Ziggy Stardust.

Sydney, Australia
FOREVER YOURS
Heroes/What In The World/Be My Wife/ Jean Genie/Blackout/Art Decade/ Breaking Glass/Fame/Beauty And The Beast/Five Years/Star/Hang Onto Yourself/Ziggy Stardust/Suffragette City/ Instrumental/Rebel, Rebel/Alabama Song/Station To Station/TVC-15/Stay

Adelaide, November 11
SPEED OF LIFE
Five Years/Soul Love/Star/Hang Onto Yourself/Ziggy Stardust/Suffragette City/ Alabama Song/Station To Station/ TVC-15/Stay/Rebel, Rebel

As will be seen from the song list the Melbourne tape is incomplete and that Sydney contains the most complete concert; certainly more complete than the Official 'tour album' which, while including a couple of the older numbers looks more towards the newer material, and as such doesn't really represent what the tour was all about... Bowie proving that not only could he still belt out the old songs the way we all loved them but that he was more into the electronic age and was quite happy thank you very much. 'Stage' just shows the determination of Bowie to soldier on not giving more than a nod to his raunchier days... an impression, which looked at in the light of the bootlegs, is totally wrong.

AN EVENING WITH DAVID BOWIE
Radio Superstars
RCA DJL-1 3016
Promotion Interview Album
Ziggy Stardust/Station To Station/ Beauty And The Beast/Fame

Recorded in David's apartment 'high above the streets of New York City' with Sonny Fox this promo album covers the years from the release of 'Low', with David explaining how he had always felt that he was interested in the remoteness of the new music writing and how he had always felt that he wasn't competent to break into the neo-avantgardism of the new style when he had first heard it in London with Daevid Allen and Gong and Kevin Ayres, but that his good friend Eno had lent him a shoulder to lean on and given him the impetus to experiment (that experiment being 'Low').

He was aware that he might lose a few of the fans who had picked up on him during the Young Americans period who might not be aware that he changed from album to album and that he might lose them but that was a calculated risk.

'I'm not creating narrative from albums at the moment. It started off as an experiment but I can see it continuing as long as the initial spark of excitement continues and when it leaves I'll move on' David says but realises that his use of electronics is as a texture. 'If I see the need for a synthesiser I'll use it but I won't use it where I need a guitar sound... if I need that I'll use a guitar, but then I may mistreat it by putting it through a synth, but if I need to create a new sound I'll use the synthesiser'.

Sonny Fox then asks David about Tommy Newton in The Man Who Fell To Earth, and Nick Roeg 'I stopped trying to define the film but played the part the way Nick wanted to do it... I wanted to see the way a director reacts with an actor... the character in the book is the sort of character I was playing on stage remote'. David then goes on to say that he doesn't have a technical attribute in his head and that he couldn't possibly direct a film from the technical point of view.

Somehow the conversation comes around to the Diamond Dogs tour and how Bowie had sold the tour out on the principle of the special effects but by the time the tour had hit LA he was bored with it and had gone soul.

Passing on from music he mentions in passing his neo-fascist phase and how it was misunderstood... What he had been trying to do when he arrived in London that time was to show how (theatrically) a charismatic figure could encapsulate the feeling behind the National Front in the UK and show them up for what they are... but it all back-fired and the press and public thought that he was trying to push himself into the political arena. He said that fascism and the National Front are the last refuge of idiots.

Moving away from all of these 'heavy' subjects he talked about his travels, to Thailand and South Cambodia, Japan and his search for the light (a return to Buddhism except that when he returned from the mountain he modelled an ad for Saki!) and a visit to Africa where he went on a safari (the type where the bearers carry the baggage on their heads!) he

speaks a little about the Masai tribe with whom he spent a few hours, but didn't come to grips with their culture.

In all the promo album covers too many subjects in too short a time but does give a few prompts towards the next official album.

LIVE IN STOCKHOLM 1979
Audifon (Germany)
Secret Life Of Arabia/Heroes/What In The World/Be My Wife
Jean Genie/Blackout/Speed Of Life/Breaking Glass
Fame/Beauty And The Beast/Five Years/Soul Love/Star
Hang Onto Yourself/Ziggy Stardust/Art Decade/Suffragette City/Alabama Song/Station To Station.

Nassau, NY
RESURRECTION ON 84TH STREET
Station To Station/Suffragette City/Fame
Stay/Panic In Detroit
Changes/TVC 15/Diamond Dogs

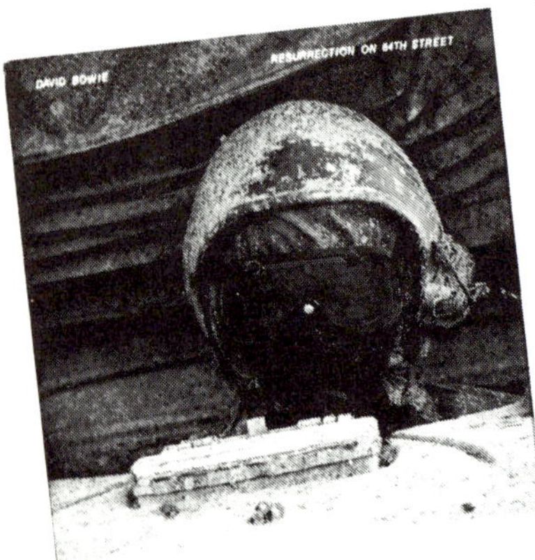

Word On A Wing/Jean Genie
Musicians: David Bowie, Carlos Alomar, Stacy Heydon, George Murray, Tony Kay, Dennis Davis
Producer: Jim Gilmore
A very high quality bootleg from the US tour.

March 1979
I PITY THE FOOL/TAKE MY TIP YOU'VE GOT A HABIT OF LEAVING/ BABY LOVES THAT WAY
EMI NUT EP EMI 2925
Producer: Shel Talmy
A tasteful re-release from EMI,

April 1979
BOYS KEEP SWINGING/ FANTASTIC VOYAGE
RCA BOW 2 (UK)
Producers: David Bowie, Tony Visconti

Contrary to his statement in the Superstars interview that he was going to continue experimenting with electronic music David released this single in advance of the album.

With an almost total return to pop 'Boys' brings back the sexually ambiguous theme from the Ziggy days; boys have a lot of fun... you can wear a uniform, buy a home of your own, learn to drive and everything... it's a very confusing song since all of the things boys can do are laid out with just a trace of machismo, yet there's an underlying camp (of the Village People YMCA type).

The song was recorded by putting all of the musicians onto different instruments than those they normally play, Carlos Alomar on drums when he usually plays guitar, etc. The result is a slightly amateur sound which works surprisingly well with the lyrics (the obvious drum-beat for instance).

May 1979
LODGER
RCA BOW LP 1 (UK)/RCA AQL1 3254
Fantastic Voyage/African Night Flight/Move On/Yassassin/Red Sails/DJ/Look Back In Anger/Boys Keep Swinging/Repetition/Red Money
Producers: David Bowie, Tony Visconti
Musicians: David Bowie, Tony Visconti, Carlos Alomar, Dennis Davis, Brian Eno, Adrian Belew, Simon House, Roger Powell, Sean Mayes, George Murray.

With the single climbing the charts slowly RCA issued the new album which was a showcase of the best tracks from a 22 track tape which Bowie and Eno had recorded.

It's Bowie's most narrative album for some time, while not quite a return to his old style of concept records, each song must be taken separately although it is easy to see where each has come from if the album is taken in conjunction with the Superstars interview record.

'Fantastic Voyage' is a reasonably straightforward number about the dignity of life and the threat of the atomic bomb hanging over us all... learning to live with somebody's depression. But as Bowie says: 'It veers off to the obscure... One feels constantly that so many things are out of our own control and it's just this infuriating, that you don't want their depression ruling your life or dictating how you will wake up every morning!'

The next track, 'African Night Flight' is about his visit to Kenya on safari, where he met these German 'exiles' who had been away from the fatherland for seventeen years and spent their time hopping about in light aircraft, getting very drunk and talking about going 'home' on leave... infused into this basic theme are little Zen phrases about flying into the eye of God on high, and a mention of the wise orangutang (if you refer to the inside sleeve you'll find a Thai Buddhist temple). Bowie claims that 'Move On' is blatantly romantic (back to his theme of being a traveller... or a lodger), and is almost a Cook's tour of where he went on his holidays. Musically it has an interesting history... he was playing around with a Revox tape recorder and a tape got twisted... he felt that backwards it sounded good and copied the original song down note for note backwards and played it onto another tape, and the basic melody line of 'Move On' came out... the original twisted tape had been playing 'All The Young Dudes'... an interesting experiment.

'Yassassin' is Bowie's tribute to Jamaican music and Turkish culture. With Simon House, ex of Hawkwind, on violin Bowie fused reggae and Turkish music to come up with this very strange culture clash which surprisingly works very well. Lyrically David says that it's about the sort of guy you see around the coffee bars in Turkey.

The scene is somewhere in the South China Sea and an English swashbuckling pirate Erroll Flyn type moves about offering his services to whoever will pay. That's the basic storyline for 'Red Sails' as David emulated Japanese music to the point of overdoing it.

On side two 'Look Back In Anger' is a vague track about the tatty angel of death and doesn't really make much sense. The style of recording the track was a little strange too; a blackboard with chords on it was placed in front of the musicians and Eno pointed to the chord he wanted them to play, after thirty minutes of this it was so intense that it was ready to be recorded... 'Fortunately I'm with guys who are very receptive to what I want to do. They get angry, of course, but only if they're not fully aware of what is going on,' said Bowie.

'Repetition' is the most direct song on the album, wife beating is a common occurrence throughout the world and this song tries to show why it happens without glorifying it: Johnny is a man and he's bigger than her, I guess the bruises won't show if she wears long sleeves!

'Red Money' is back to the almost nonsense lyric which Bowie seems to revel in these days, he went some way towards explaining it in an interview by saying that red boxes seem to keep appearing in his paintings . . . but it doesn't really explain it at all!

The cover is interesting, a postcard featuring Bowie pinned against a tiled wall... but inside images conflict; Che Guevara being shown off by the Bolivian police after he had been riddled with bullets in 1967 sits on the same collage with Buddha and a picture of Bowie being made-up for the cover pic... a strange combination.

Following the release of the album, Bowie took himself off into semi seclusion only coming out to do a short promotion film for the Kenny Everett Video Show screened on ITV in the UK... his choice of song for the Christmas Special was strange: 'Space Oddity'!

Featuring Bowie in a dentist's chair in the middle of a studio kitchen which as the song progresses begins blowing up appliance by appliance, fridge first then cooker, toaster, mixers et al. A very strange sequence which turned out to be a little more dangerous than Bowie anticipated, since one of the exploding appliances actually showered him with sparks and he received minor burns – not too serious though.

June 1979
DJ/REPETITION
RCA BOW 3 (UK)
DJ/FANTASTIC VOYAGE
RCA PB 1161 (US)
Producers: David Bowie, Tony Visconti

DJ is very much Bowie's rejection of his Disco days. 'It's a somewhat cynical song, but it's my natural response to disco. The DJ is the one who is having the ulcers now, not the executives, because if you do the unthinkable thing of putting a record on in a disco not in time... that's it. If you have thirty seconds silence, your whole career is over'... well that's a slight exaggeration of the situation, it doesn't work quite like that.

It is strange that musically he didn't go over the top with disco-music for this track but played it very laid back mid-seventies disco style.

The intro, those four notes on the viola came out of a gig at Carnegie Hall where David had been invited onstage to play with John Cale, he learned the four notes for the gig and transferred them to the song... 'I may learn another four and play them on my next album'.

December 1979
JOHN I'M ONLY DANCING (AGAIN)
(1975)**/JOHN I'M ONLY DANCING**
(1972)
RCA BOW 4 (UK)
JOHN I'M ONLY DANCING (AGAIN)/ GOLDEN YEARS
RCA PD L1886 (US)
Producers: David Bowie, Tony Visconti
These releases were available as both 7″ and 12″ platters, and the (Again) was added to indicate a version recorded at Sigma Sound in Philadelphia during the Young Americans sessions.

February 1980
ALABAMA SONG/SPACE ODDITY
RCA BOW 5 (UK)
Producers: David Bowie, Tony Visconti
The A side – by Berthold Brecht and Kurt Weil – had been featured live during David's 1978 World Tour but this version was a studio recording, and a mighty depressing three and a half minutes at that. This version of 'Space Oddity' was recorded with acoustic guitar accompaniment only and featured on video as part of Kenny Everett's New Year's Eve TV show on December 31, 1979.

Shortly after the show David was seen in a London record store buying up a stock of albums including some Elvis Costello and attracting more than passing glances from the rest of the megastore's customers . . . the rumour was abroad that he would be recording a new album in London, the first for many years.

August 1980
ASHES TO ASHES/MOVE ON
RCA BOW 6 (UK)
ASHES TO ASHES/IT'S NO GAME
RCA PB 12078 (US)
Producers: David Bowie, Tony Visconti
This single (backed by a track from the

Lodger album) contains the message 'Produced by David Bowie and Tony Visconti from the forthcoming album Scary Monsters'.

The single went into the charts at No 4 and within two weeks had made the number 1 spot.

It seems to be the laying of the Bowie ghost of 'Space Oddity' ten years later, David is telling us that Major Tom's a junkie while there's an eerie voice fading in giving it a sort of requiem feel.

The promo-film is another strange affair (well whatdya expect) with Bowie dressed in clown suit, white face and pointed hat (see the record sleeve). The camera flashes back to the dreaded exploding kitchen with Bowie sitting in the dentist's chair but this time he's not singing 'Space Oddity' but 'Ashes To Ashes' . . . and then it's back up to date to a beach landscape pathed in red as Bowie and assorted backup vocalists lead a funeral procession with the rear being brought up by a bulldozer.

True to form David was in the US ignoring the release of the single by taking the part of the deformed John Merrick in a play in Denver, Colorado called 'The Elephant Man' which grossed a staggering $186,466 in its first week at the Denver Centre of Performing Arts, making it the centre's biggest box office take in its 38 year history.

The play went on to fare equally well over a month-long engagement in Chicago, and a three-month season in New York.

August 1980
CRYSTAL JAPAN/ALABAMA SONG
RCA SS 3270 (Japan)
Producers: David Bowie, Tony Visconti
Released only in Japan, this single was

used (with Bowie's consent) to promote a brand of Japanese Saki rice wine. It was recorded during the sessions that resulted in Scary Monsters but left off the album.

September 1980
SCARY MONSTERS (AND SUPER CREEPS)
RCA BOW LP2 (UK)/
RCA AQL 13647 (US)
It's No Game (No 1)/Up The Hill Backwards/Scary Monsters (And Super Creeps)/Ashes To Ashes/Fashion Teenage Wildlife/Scream Like A Baby/ Kingdom Come/Because You're Young/ It's No Game (No 2)
Producers: David Bowie, Tony Visconti
Musicians: David Bowie, Dennis Davis, George Murray, Carlos Alomar, Chuck Hammer, Robert Fripp, Roy Bittan, Andy Clark, Pete Townshend, Tony Visconti, Lynn Maitland, Chris Porter, Michi Hirota.

Recorded at the Power Station by Bowie and Visconti (they aren't credited as producers, the credit reads simply 'Recorded by David Bowie and Tony Visconti) this new album is a departure from the electronic overkill of 'Low' and 'Heroes', a stage further than 'Lodger' in his return to the narrative concept album. Having said that this is not a return to the 'Ziggy Stardust' or 'Diamond Dogs' days, there is no story line but there is a similarity to 'Diamond Dogs' in that the 'revolution' is happening now, and not sometime in the future, the packs of dogs are on the streets of Britain's cities, teenage kids, unemployed and angry, and this seems to be Bowie's album for them. This is not exactly a new idea, Pink Floyd did it nine months before with 'The Wall'; Pete Townshend, who plays guitar on 'Because You're Young', had a hit with his new-wavey 'Rough Boys' but perhaps the Sex Pistols did it better than anyone in 1976 with 'Pretty Vacant' and 'Anarchy In The UK' – less melodic than the others mentioned, less musical, and totally unprofessional, but a more accurate picture of what the kids on the street corners, with nothing to do, feel about life. But Bowie, Townshend and Floyd don't emulate the days of punk but reflect it through their eyes of experience – or preaching dull boring old farts as no doubt the actual frustrated teenage unemployed on the actual street corners will claim.
The first track, 'It's No Game (No 1)', opens with some obscure mechanical noises before actually starting, then it's into a Japanese translation of the English lyrics by Hisahi Miura spat out Samurai-style (as Bowie puts it) by Michi Hirota, after the first verse Bowie comes in with the English lyrics hoarsely screamed. The lyrics are very direct (as many of them are on the album) he leaves no doubt about what he's talking about; the growing fascism, 'the revolution' the whole basis of the song is that it is no game, we're playing for real now, they break fingers in Chile, starving refugees on TV, and the violence on the street. He contrasts the 'harmlessness' of throwing a rock which breaks into pieces with picking up a gun against oppression, the latter makes the papers ... although the object is the same; to hurt.

Continuing with the theme 'Up The Hill Backwards' puts forward an existential view of this 'freedom' which we are supposed to have, it may well be no game, but there's bugger all we can do about it, it has nothing to do with us the world keeps turning, we sleep together and it's just like going up hill backwards.

'Scary Monsters' is an introduction to the 'drug experience' and the destruction of the mind with the 'faster' drugs which Bowie admits he has a penchant for. It's a fast manic track with all of the implied paranoia, brought on particularly by Fripp's guitar. 'Scary Monsters' prefaces the single 'Ashes To Ashes' well, and hearing it in context it's an incredibly revealing track throwing up many questions about his earlier work and just how he held it all together.

It's back to the main theme after that little sidetrack – 'Fashion' ends the album side so you don't forget what we're really talking about – it would appear that the kids are dressing up and roaming the streets in a dance of death, tension and fear. Look to the Mods, the Punks, Skinheads, Clockwork Orange clones, Hitler Youth/Blackshirts and, yes, even the Ziggy lookalikes, they are all in the goon squad. But turning to the extremes of the Right (and Left) they aren't on their own, they don't pick these things up out of thin air; it's the ones from good homes who are doing the talking this year 'and it's loud and it's tasteless'. Yes folks it's our popular heroes of the press and TV the leaders; Reagan, Thatcher, Webster, Pinochet, Franco, and Hitler all tell us when to turn which way to turn and what to shout while we're on the dance floor. 'Listen to me – talk to me – dance with me... don't dance with me'.

Bowie said that this song was for a mythical younger brother, it's certainly for his younger followers... he seems to be finally exorcising the spectre of fascism which seemed to have attached itself to his coat tails.

There's a feeling of 'Heroes' about the first track on side two, 'Teenage Wildlife', the phrasing of the guitar, the rhythm and the overall vocal style. That seems to be in perfect sympathy with the lyrics which could be a scathing attack on the Bowie-clones like Gary Numan the New Wave Boys playing the same old thing in brand new drag... but Davey baby isn't going to play that game, he's not a piece of teenage wildlife anymore – he's thirty two now f'rchrissakes!

'Scream Like A Baby' is perhaps the most obscure of the tracks on this album, police oppression, racial prejudice, and the funny farm rehabilitation centres cow the narrator, but Sam wouldn't take it and become part of the society, he lay in the back of the police car spitting in their eyes and screaming like a baby... it seems to be telling us not to submit.

The inclusion of a Tom Verlaine track on the album is a minor break with the Bowie rock-singer-songwriter tradition, but it fits into the general theme. 'Kingdom Come' started easing its way onto the album when Carlos Alomar suggested that it might be a good idea to do a cover-version of it. Until then David had never considered recording with Verlaine, but had had some thoughts about working with him.

'Because You're Young' is Bowie's advice to his son Zowie, it's not a picture of the world through rose coloured glasses as in Kooks the 'lovers story' has ended; Angie and David have been divorced and there's just a hint of an explanation about this update. It is almost embarrassing attempting to work out what he's talking about since there's this feeling that the song is highly personal; 'she took back everything she said and left him nearly out of his mind', so he'll just dance his life away, with a million dreams and a million scars!

The album ends with a slow dancing version of 'It's No Game (No 2), this time without the Samurai lady or the hoarse voice.

October 1978
FASHION/SCREAM LIKE A BABY
RCA BOW T7 (UK)/RCA PB 12134 (US)
Producers: Tony Visconti, David Bowie

December, 1980
THE BEST OF DAVID BOWIE
K-Tel NE 1111 (UK)
Space Oddity/Life On Mars/Starman/ Rock 'n' Roll Suicide/John I'm Only Dancing/Jean Genie/Breaking Glass/ Sorrow/Diamond Dogs/Young Americans/Fame/Golden Years/TVC 15/ Sound And Vision/Heroes/Boys Keep Swinging
Producers: Various
Capitalising on the extraordinary success of Scary Monsters and the concurrent rise of the New Romantic movement (which was greatly indebted to Bowie), K-Tel leased these tracks (David's top 16 singles) from RCA and, following an expensive TV advertising campaign, the album was a big seller.

January 1981
SCARY MONSTERS (AND SUPER CREEPS)/BECAUSE YOU'RE YOUNG
RCA BOW 8 (UK)
Producers: David Bowie, Tony Visconti
Continuing RCA's tradition of milking album, this track was the third to be taken from Scary Monsters and, inevitably, it stiffed as a single. It was also made available in cassette form.

May 1981
CHRISTIANE F. WIR KINDER VOM BAHNHOF ZOO
RCA BL 43606 (Germany)
V-2 Schneider/TVC 15/Heroes/Boys Keep Swinging/Sense Of Doubt
Station To Station/Look Back In Anger/ Stay/Warszawa
Producers: David Bowie, Tony Visconti (except TVC 15 and Stay – David Bowie and Harry Maslin)
David's music was selected for the soundtrack of this German film (English translation: The Children of Bahnhof Zoo) which deals with teenage drug addiction. It also featured David performing in a Berlin discotheque. RCA Germany released this soundtrack album which was imported into England by the domestic branch of RCA. Some 25,000 were imported.

Bowie seems to have finally come to grips with electronic music and his lyrical experimentation; having gone through 'Heroes', 'Low' and even 'Lodger' to get to the point where he is now, and it seems like not a bad place to be. Sometimes what he's doing is way over the top in its obscurity and other times it is about as obvious as his ex-wife's 'kiss and tell' story in the trashy tabloids (like the repetitive synth riff on the track 'Scary Monsters' which is more than reminiscent of Joni Mitchell's 'Jungle Line') but on the whole David seems to have put the weirdness aside and is trying to make out in this world as a thirty year old with a nine year old son.

The days of rebellion, the London Boys, Ziggy, Aladdin etc, are still there slinking about in the background waiting to be called upon, but these days he doesn't call them up too often.

November 1981
UNDER PRESSURE/SOUL BROTHER
EMI 5250 (UK)/Elektra/
Asylum E 47235 (US)

An unlikely one-off partnership between Bowie and Queen who happened to be using the same studio in Montreux, Switzerland, at the same time. Bowie wrote and produced the A side which features him duetting with Queen's Freddie Mercury and backed by the rest of Queen. As well as being a sizeable hit, it demonstrated most effectively the superior emotive quality of Bowie's voice. The flipside features Queen alone.

February 1982
BAAL EP
Baal's Hymn/Remembering Marie A/ Ballad Of The Adventurers/The Drowned Girl/The Dirty Song
RCA BOW 11 (UK)
RCA CP2 14346 (US)
Producers: Tony Visconti, David Bowie

All titles by Bertolt Brecht and Dominic Muldowney with the exception of 'The Drowned Girl' by Bertolt Brecht and Kurt Weill.

With music taking a back seat in favour of thespian endeavour, RCA's only new Bowie release of 1982 was this far from commercial collection of songs taken from the TV film of Brecht's first play in which Bowie acted the title role. The austere music was hardly likely to attract radio play but the package was presented in an attractive fold-out sleeve with stills from the play and a synopsis of the plot.

November 1982
SPACE ODDITY/CHANGES/ VELVET GOLDMINE
RCA BOWP 101
LIFE ON MARS/THE MAN WHO SOLD THE WORLD
RCA BOWP 102
THE JEAN GENIE/ZIGGY STARDUST
RCA BOWP 103
REBEL REBEL/QUEEN BITCH
RCA BOWP 104
SOUND AND VISION/A NEW CAREER IN A NEW TOWN
RCA BOWP 105
DRIVE IN SATURDAY/ROUND AND ROUND
RCA BOWP 106
SORROW/AMSTERDAM
RCA BOWP 107
GOLDEN YEARS/CAN YOU HEAR ME
RCA BOWP 108
BOYS KEEP SWINGING/ FANTASTIC VOYAGE
RCA BOWP 109
ASHES TO ASHES/MOVE ON
RCA BOWP 110
Produced variously by Ken Scott, Tony Visconti, David Bowie.

Released under the collective title of 'Fashions' and packaged in a plastic binder with decorative photography, this was a limited edition (25,000) set of picture singles designed to illustrate Bowie's influence on rock music. All ten singles were top ten hits in the UK and all ten are re-issued with their original B sides. They were the first picture discs to feature Bowie and the pictures themselves illustrate the artist at appropriate chronological stages in his career. While cynics might suggest that RCA were milking an already spent barrel, the set was aimed at collectors and made an imaginative, quality package.

November 1982
PEACE ON EARTH/LITTLE DRUMMER BOY/FANTASTIC VOYAGE
RCA BOW 12 (UK)/
RCA PH 13400 (US)
Producers: Tony Visconti, David Bowie

The two tracks on the first side of this seasonal release feature Bowie duetting with Bing Crosby with whom he appeared in an American TV special in November 1977. The venerable old crooner died shortly after the taping and the special was brought forward as a result (see page 61). 'Fantastic Voyage' is one of the better tracks from the 'Lodger' LP.

January 1983
BOWIE RARE
RCA PL 45406
Ragazzo Solo, Ragazza Sola/'Round and 'Round/Amsterdam/Holy Holy/ Panic In Detroit/Young Americans/ Velvet Goldmine/Helden/John, I'm Only Dancing (Again) (1975)/Moon Of Alabama/Crystal Japan (instrumental)
Producers: Gus Dudgeon, Ken Scott, Tony Visconti, David Bowie.

Bowie's final album on RCA – future compilations aside – was compiled by RCA Italy which may explain why the Italian speaking version of 'Space Oddity' opens the programme. The title is a misnomer insofar as any

respectable Bowie collector would already possess the majority of tracks but here's a short run down on their origins:

Ragazzo Solo, Ragazza Sola: The Italian version of 'Space Oddity' (see page 20) was a big local hit in 1969 and probably inspired Ken Pitt to enter Bowie in an Italian song festival the same year.

'Round And 'Round: A great version of the Chuck Berry standard originally used as the B side for 'Drive In Saturday' (see page 35.) Recorded with The Spiders, it was rumoured to have been scheduled for inclusion on the 'Ziggy Stardust' LP.

Amsterdam: A rather gloomy Jacques Brel piece originally released as the B side to 'Sorrow' (see page 38).

Holy Holy: A 1971 single (see page 24) and also the B side of 'Diamond Dogs' (see page 40).

Panic In Detroit: An inferior live version of the 'Aladdin Sane' cut recorded at the same time as the 'David Live' LP but left off the album and used as the B side to Bowie's live 'Knock On Wood' single (see page 42).

Young Americans: This is the re-mixed and generally superior version which was released in the US and is considerably shorter than the more familiar UK single and album versions (see page 47).

Helden: The song 'Heroes' was originally recorded in English, German and French and on the German LP cut Bowie sings the first half in English and the second in German. This is the version included here (see page 60). The identical track, incidentally, was included on the 'Bahnhof Zoo' soundtrack collection released in Germany (and imported into the UK) in 1981 (see page 80).

John, I'm Only Dancing (Again) (1975): This is the Sigma Sound 'Young Americans' session re-make of the 1972 single which was first issued in 1979 (backed with the original single version) on 12″ and 7″ discs (see page 75). Like the 7″ disc, it has been edited from its original six minutes plus to 3 minutes and 27 seconds.

Moon Of Alabama: Also known as The Alabama Song, this unmelodious Brecht-Weill song was coupled with a sparse re-recording of Space Oddity and released as a single in 1980 (see page 75).

Crystal Japan: A Japanese-only release (RCA SS 3270), this instrumental was used as a jingle to promote Saki in 1980. Questionable aesthetics aside, it is the only track on the album that is a genuine collectors' item.

April 1983
LET'S DANCE/CAT PEOPLE (PUTTING OUT FIRE)
EMI EA 152 (UK)/EMI 8158 (US)
Producers: David Bowie, Nile Rodgers

With timing as precise as a watch from his chosen country of residence, Bowie re-emerges with a new label, a commercial sound and a publicity campaign that raised his profile to heights not seen since the mid-seventies. Promoted by a series of intriguing videos, 'Let's Dance' ascended rapidly and deservedly to number one in the UK singles chart and signalled the start to what will probably become the most lucrative period in Bowie's long career.

April 1983
LET'S DANCE
EMI AML 3029 (UK)/
EMI ST 17093 (US)

Modern Love/China Girl/Let's Dance/ Without You/Ricochet/Criminal World/ Cat People (Putting Out Fire)/Shake It
Producers: David Bowie, Nile Rodgers.

When EMI released two singles by Bowie in 1965, no-one could have guessed that 18 years later the same company would fork out a reported $17.5 million to secure his signature for a second time. In return he presented them with his most commercial work in a decade and arguably the most enjoyable listening experience of his entire career. The album blends many styles of music but hits hardest with the sleek rhythm and blues songs like the title track 'Ricochet' and – best of all – 'Modern Love' which opens side one. The latter may have been subconsciously derived from 'Tell Him', the 1963 Billie David hit, but its astonishing momentum and irresistible hook line make it the most outstanding cut on the LP. Not far behind is the new version of Bowie and Georgio Moroder's 'Cat People (Putting Out Fire)' which features some unusually tasty guitar work by Stevie Ray Vaughn and is the best hard rock number Bowie has recorded in years. Not surprisingly the album followed the single to the top of the charts and concurrent announcements of a world tour have placed Bowie firmly in the spotlight once again.

The new deal with EMI will presumably allow Bowie to utilise the company's extensive film and video involvements. During the hiatus from recording in 1982 Bowie made two films, Merry Christmas Mr Lawrence and The Hunger, neither of which had gone on release at the time of writing. The first named was directed by Nagisa Ashima and is a study of prisoners and captors in a Japanese POW camp in Java in 1942 in which Bowie plays a tough officer who refuses to break under torture. Co-starring Catherine Deneuve, The Hunger is a horror epic in which Bowie is cast as a 300 year old man.